MILLIONAIRE
MAINTENANCE MAN

ROB LANE

MILLIONAIRE

MAINTENANCE MAN

ROB LANE

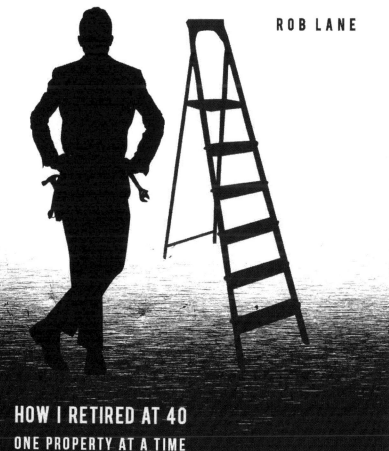

HOW I RETIRED AT 40

ONE PROPERTY AT A TIME

This book is lovingly dedicated to my mom,
whose unconditional love and commitment
to raising her children was her greatest
source of achievement.

You taught me how to be a better person;
it is a privilege to be your son...

TABLE OF CONTENTS

SECTION 1

SECTION 2

SECTION 3

SECTION 1

IS THIS BOOK FOR YOU?

—◄ ►—

I WROTE THIS BOOK TO TELL YOU MY STORY. I want you to see that anything is possible. It doesn't matter from where you came. It doesn't matter under what conditions you were raised. The only thing that really matters is what you want to accomplish and your willingness to do what it takes to get what you want.

This book isn't about being an overnight success. It's about a method I've used to create wealth. I'm talking about the kind of wealth that allowed me to retire from the normal work force at 40 years of age. I was no overnight success unless you consider 20 years of persistence and hard work to be overnight.

I really can't think of a time when I've actually heard of an overnight success. People who reach success typically spend years gaining the knowledge and experience that allowed them to become successful. Anyone I know, that has achieved success, has built it over a period of time. They've had challenges and failures just like you and I.

Challenges and failures are part of life. No matter what you do, you are going to have good times and bad. You're going to have successes and failures. The successful people I've met have all dealt with the same circumstances.

The big difference in every case is that, successful people learn from their failures and build on their successes. The most important trait I've witnessed in every successful person I've ever met is action. Successful people take action. They don't always wait and figure it all out. They have an idea and if it's something they can implement, they take action and do it.

My hope is that this book will help you find ideas that you can take action on right away. I hope that you get ideas and inspiration to implement some of those ideas. Reading this book or any other real estate or finance book will not make you an expert, as "academia" would have you believe...you've got to get your nose bloodied.

This book is about working hard and being disciplined with your money and time. It's about what

MILLIONAIRE MAINTENANCE MAN

can be done with a solid plan of action and discipline. The business model I'm going to share with you requires discipline, hard work, and persistence.

This is not a get rich quick deal; it's a long-term solution. This book gives you a way to build and grow your wealth in any economy. If you're looking for shortcuts to wealth and financial independence, this book isn't for you.

If you're interested, and being a full-time weekend warrior appeals to you, this book may be the answer you're looking for.

The proof that this system works is all around you. Almost anywhere you go there are people making a good living and building their wealth with income producing property. It's a proven wealth building strategy that works now just like it did 300 years ago. The proof is in the number of individual family homes being rented in virtually any market.

This book is about how I started with absolutely nothing and became a millionaire with income producing property. This story tells how I used the only asset I had to grow my income. That asset was my ability to out-work most anyone else. So I out worked everyone around me to grow my income.

Working hard and growing my income allowed me to start investing in income producing properties. Buying income-producing properties enabled me to build a business that continues to provide growing cash flow.

That cash flow has given me the ability to leave the corporate world. Now I focus on what I love: buying single-family homes, making them beautiful, and then renting them for premium rate rental income.

I'm going to give you every tool from my toolbox that you will need to kick start your own program. I will give you tools like downloadable contracts, lease applications, eviction notices, and service checklists. It will be everything you need to start building your assets and growing your cash flow.

This book is both my story and my business model. I don't leave much out and sometimes the details are a little scary. I want you to see from where I came. I'm going to show you the challenges I faced and how I overcame those challenges. I want you to understand that if I can do it, so can you. I want you to see the mistakes I made in hopes that you don't make the same.

There are plenty of books on buying and managing rental property. Most of them will give you a completely different business plan than the one I'm going to show you. Many of these books will talk about the basics. Some will talk about the nuts and bolts only. This book was written to give you everything you need to do this for yourself.

Let's talk about a mindset, a way of thinking. Mindset is a critical ingredient in any successful business. I want you to get a feel for that mindset because it's the core of every success from which I've been blessed.

I'm not saying this book is the end all cure all for someone wanting to get into income producing property. In fact, I recommend that you read everything you can get your hands on about the topic. Knowledge is power when action is taken on that knowledge. So read, talk to professionals, join forums, and ask questions. Just make sure that you take action on what you learn and your odds of success will be great.

My intention is to give you all the information I can so you are inspired to take action and start building your own financial legacy. Build a legacy that you can pass on to your children and they can pass on to their children.

This book is the ideal solution for the young person just getting started. I started down this path at 20 years of age and have never looked back. It doesn't really matter what age you are or where you are in life.

You can use this business to increase your wealth and cash flow. The information in this book can help you make a drastic change in your financial life.

Regardless of where you are in life, you have the power to change your financial picture. If the idea of designing your financial future rather than living your life by someone else's design makes sense to you, you're in the right place.

If you're ready, let's roll up our sleeves and get this party started.

SECTION 2

MY STORY

IT IS MY HOPE THAT MY STORY WILL MOTIVATE you to take whatever action is needed to help move you to the next level. Only you can decide what that "next level" is.

I want you to see for yourself from where I came. I want you to know the obstacles I had to overcome. It's important for you to see that I was not born into wealth. In fact, I was born into poverty.

The reason this is important is to illustrate that no matter where you come from and no matter what obstacles you have to overcome, there is always light at the end of the tunnel. I hope this can serve as an inspiration to you.

Action is always the answer to moving forward in life. If you take positive action you will succeed. My hope is to motivate you to take action in your life. Action needs to be taken to help move you to the next level.

Only you can decide what that next level is. Then you can figure out what would be the appropriate action. Most people seem to spend their lives getting in the way of what they want instead of just taking that next step.

If my story can help give you an idea of what that next step is and motivates you to take action, then I have accomplished what I set out to do in writing this book.

So let's get started...

NO POSTER CHILD FOR SUCCESS

ANYONE THAT KNEW ME WHEN I WAS YOUNG wouldn't have predicted my success. I had too many obstacles in the way. The odds were never going to be in my favor. At least that's the way it would've appeared.

The life I was born into was a breeding ground for perpetual poverty. I grew up in a small town in rural Oklahoma and was raised by my mother and two older sisters. My parents were divorced before I was a year old and I didn't see much of my father until years later.

My mother had my oldest sister when she was 13 years of age and my other sister when she was 17. I was born when my mom was 21, as a last ditch effort to save a failing marriage.

My mom was tall and beautiful. She remarried a couple of times during my childhood years, but they never lasted long. With the exception of my wife, my mother was the strongest, most independent woman I've ever known.

As I stated earlier, my real father wasn't in the picture when I was growing up. He started coming around during high school when college scouts began to recruit me to play college football. He made it to many of my high school football games, but as time went on, we found we didn't have much in common. That relationship eventually dissolved, but I'm okay with that.

I remember doing without because there was never any child support from my father. My mother didn't deserve the cards she was dealt when left to raise three children by herself.

There are memories that no child should have to endure. Like the time my mother had to file bankruptcy on her beauty shop. Yes, my mother was also an entrepreneur. She was a hairdresser by trade and owned her own beauty shop when she was 30. She was responsible for developing the work ethic in my sisters and myself, but nothing will erase the memory of the day the repo man came and took our television and VCR.

That work ethic is what would eventually ensure that her children wouldn't have to live the same kind of life that she did. Unfortunately, she never had the opportunity to develop her financial intelligence. Throughout this book you'll see me refer to financial intelligence. It's a term I use to describe a way of thinking about money and how to use and handle it.

My mother made a decent living but managed to spend her money as fast as she made it. She was also an inventor. When we were kids, we thought her invention was going to make us rich but that never happened.

My sisters and I grew up living in crappy little rent houses. We dreamed of someday owning our own homes. We all wanted our share of the American dream.

When I was 17 my mother remarried. She found another kind of happiness and spent the best years of her life with my stepfather, to whom I'm still close. My mother passed away at the young age of 59 from cancer. Her life was so difficult yet she always held her head high.

I remember my mother coming home after working a 12-hour day and putting together an entertainment center with a butter knife. She mowed her own yard. Since we couldn't afford a weed eater, we had to cut the fence line grass with a pair of scissors. In spite of the conditions, my mother was a proud woman. We may have lived in a crappy little rent house but the yard and flowers were always impeccable.

She would make sure that my sisters and I were always well dressed. I'll never forget her taking me on dates, just Mom and son. She did that so she could teach me what chivalry in a gentleman looked like and to always be the one to give the right of way to whomever crossed my path. The woman carried a cane fishing pole in our car so that if we happened by a body of water, she could be the male role model to her only son. I'm still a big fisherman to this day.

She was a mentor to all, and took in our stray friends that had no place to go. She had NO fear. She would always tell us, "Just because you're poor doesn't mean you can't have class." That's the way she lived her life. In her mind, it was about perception.

To my mother, circumstances didn't matter. It was important to give the perception of class and dignity. That's how she lived and she instilled that in each of her children.

So, being raised by three women, I always put the toilet seat down! I miss my mother dearly. I'm thankful for the lessons she taught me growing up. Without her I wouldn't be where I am today.

This book is dedicated to my mother. She taught my sisters and I to always hold our heads high, hold onto each other, and act with honor and dignity. She taught us the value of hard work. Most importantly, she taught us that anything is possible if you're willing to work for it.

NOT A GREAT STUDENT

——◆ ◆——

IF BEING A GOOD STUDENT WERE ESSENTIAL for success, I wouldn't have had a chance. Growing up I was anything but a good student. Both of my sisters were great students and did well in school. They were smart and both achieved college degrees. I did not graduate college; however, I was a Vice President and co-owner of a major food company by the age of 32.

I wasn't cut out to be good in school. I had a hard time paying attention in class. I spent most of my class time daydreaming and losing focus on where my attention should have been. I had some teachers and classes that managed to keep me engaged, but they were few and far between.

Even though I was a lousy student, I was a pretty good athlete. I did well playing high school football.

I even received offers to play college football. That would have been great. The problem was that colleges wanted their athletes to also do well with academics. It was a big disappointment to have football scholarship offers that I couldn't accept because I couldn't pass the ACT.

I know now that even if I had passed the ACT, the thought of spending another four or five years in a classroom was something I couldn't bear. I've never been someone who could sit for long periods of time. I'm ADD and don't do well if I can't be moving around. In a recent experience on test taking, I was sent to Minnesota for my company to understand the anatomy of poultry for a manufacturer we represented. I was mortified as I knew grades on testing would be posted for all to see. I was the youngest and most financially successful person in the class, but scored the lowest on the test. It strengthened my dislike for academia. However, I knew I could out sell anyone in the room. I only tell you this because you may think of yourself as a failure. Unless, like me, you have taken the opportunity to prove your strengths.

I never watched much television and still don't to this day. I have to be doing something. Aside from a football game now and then, television can't hold my attention. Now, I understand my lack of attention is a blessing. There were times in school it didn't feel like a blessing, but I wouldn't change it now.

In spite of my day dreaming, I managed to graduate from high school. I spent that next summer wondering what I was going to do when I grew up. Since I grew up as poor as you can get, I had to make sure I didn't end up living like that ever again. I knew I needed some kind of education to help me move toward a better life. I enrolled at a junior college and managed to do pretty well.

I made the honor roll at that junior college but hated every minute I spent in school. I remember sitting in class daydreaming. Daydreaming was a common occurrence for me during school. I kept thinking that I could start at my current age of 20 years, get in with a good company and just work harder than anyone else. That's how I'd make money. Then, by the time my friends had graduated college I'd be two or three years ahead of them in the work force.

After all, I wasn't going to have some fancy degree that would ensure a high paying job, and we all know that fancy degrees don't always mean a high paying job. I knew I needed a plan. The only plan I could come up with was to out work everyone else. It wasn't a sexy plan, but it was a pretty good plan.

While I was in college, I worked for a retail food broker. That job entailed going around to retailers and cleaning and re-setting grocery store shelves and displays. The job wasn't glamorous but it gave me a little experience in the brokerage business. I knew this wasn't going to be a great fit for me. I figured I could use the experience to get with a better company.

I decided to put together a resume and sent it out to every food broker in the yellow pages. I managed to get two interviews and a job for my efforts. A small firm hired me at twenty years of age for $18,000 a year with a $350 a month car allowance. This company wasn't retail. They were in the food service industry, "any food away from home," which was a completely different animal.

I didn't care that I had no experience in the food service industry. It didn't matter that I didn't know the business or anything about how it worked. The only thing that mattered to me was that I got my foot in the door. Now, all I had to do was out work everyone in that company and all my dreams of a better life would come true.

You see, I knew I wasn't the smartest person in the world. I also knew I needed some kind of advantage in order to get ahead. My plan was simple. Work harder than anyone else. That's how I would stand out from the crowd and get ahead.

Within 8 months of getting that job, I was recruited and hired by a larger competitor. My starting pay jumped to $22,000 a year and a company car. I was 21 years old and I was on my way to a completely different kind of life than the one in which I grew up. I didn't know it yet, but the stage was being set for my future.

I'd been on that second job for one year and was about to turn 22 years old. That's when I found and bought my first house. It was a small duplex; each side was only 900 square feet. Half of the duplex was rented at the time. I was still living at home with my mom and stepdad. The duplex was close to downtown Oklahoma City in the arts district, and I loved it.

The area was a little sketchy, but the bones of the houses in the area were beautiful. I knew right then I had to buy it. I made an offer and bought the property. I paid $45,000 in 1994 for this duplex. My interest rate was 9.5% with a 30 year fixed mortgage.

The payment on the duplex was a little over $400 a month. The side that was rented paid $350 a month rent. I thought I was finally living the American Dream. I was 22 years old, a property owner and a landlord with a company car. My cost of living was zero, which gave me a lot of time to party. I now had my own place, and it was as nice as anything I'd lived in growing up.

At the time I had no idea what I was doing. However, the pieces of the puzzle were coming together. At 22 years old I was starting to build a portfolio of assets and income. I had a house that was almost paying for itself. I had a company car and earned income from my job and from mowing yards. This was the beginning of the mindset that would shape the rest of my life.

I remember how proud I was of what I'd accomplished. At 22 I'd already managed to step away from my childhood experiences. I'd begun to build my future. I'd worked hard and it had started paying off. The American dream was real! I was beginning to see that anyone could do it. Background and education couldn't hold me back.

As I reveled in my newfound successes, I planned to continue to do this and build something that could make me financially free. My take on being financially free means, I'm not dependent on a job to pay my bills nor do I have to purchase special insurance to pay my debts due to the loss earned income.

INCOME BUBBLES

IT'S TIME TO START TALKING ABOUT THE mindset I believe you need to build wealth. I'll get more in depth in a later chapter on how I chose to build wealth. Now, I want to share with you a philosophy that has paid me big dividends over the last twenty years.

I'm talking about a concept that I call "income bubbles". There are all kinds of names thrown around for this concept. You've probably heard it called income streams and other names. For our purposes we will call it income bubbles.

I knew when I bought my first property in 1993; I knew then I was on to something. I had a job working for a good company that paid me a salary. That was an income bubble. Then I got a better job with a better company, and I had a salary and a company car. Now,

I had two income bubbles from my job. These income bubbles were my salary, bonuses, and company car. These income bubbles fall into the category I call "earned income".

When I bought that first duplex, half was rented. The rent from that half paid a little over three hundred fifty dollars a month. That was an income bubble. Are you starting to see where I'm going with this? Creating multiple income bubbles is key to creating wealth.

So let me break this income bubble thing down for you. The first and most important income bubble is your salary or earned income from your job. You have to start somewhere, and that's where I started. I've never been handed anything. I didn't have any relatives that were a source of borrowing money to start a business. All I had was my ability to work hard and earn an income.

For this discussion I'll refer to the job income as EI or earned income. This is where it all starts for most of us. We get out of school, get a job and create EI. How you choose to manage that EI is where the rubber meets the road. This is where the entrepreneur kicks in, or at least it did for me. This is also where many of us start down the wrong path.

Too many start earning that income and try to spend it as fast as they can make it, and believe me;

I wanted to do that very same thing. So, as I tell this story, know that it was difficult not make those fancy purchases. Maybe you've fallen into this trap. The good news is there's a better plan and it's never too late to change your course.

I chose to use my EI to build something that would provide financial security down the road. At the time, I had a choice to make. I could either buy fancy cars, a nice house, and all the toys, or I could save and invest my EI in single-family homes. I chose the latter.

This is a concept that I think is important to grasp. If you're going to build something long term, you're going to have to start with your current EI. Building passive income is the goal we are trying to reach. Then as you're able to create more income bubbles, you can continue to reinvest your profits and build your passive income. It's a basic wealth building principle; you'll see it talked about in most anything you read on the subject of wealth building.

When I was 23 I was engaged to a girl I'd been dating since high school. I was still living in that first duplex but she wanted a house, not a duplex. She was going the University of Oklahoma at the time and was commuting to Norman daily for school. We found and bought a nice, two-story house in what is now a historical district of Oklahoma City.

At the same time I bought another house in Yukon (home of Garth Brooks and my current wife) that was for sale by owner. I bought these two homes back to back. They were both in bad shape and would need a lot of work. I bit off more than I could chew this time.

I tell you this story to emphasize the income bubble mind set. I was 23 years old. I had my EI, company car, and 3 rental properties. I was mowing yards and working for a contractor on other people's homes all in the name of earning extra money to reinvest in my dream of passive income (real estate acquisition). These were all income bubbles, each bubble generated income that I was able to reinvest to create more income bubbles.

There are always challenges in life and I've had my share. That fiancé and I didn't work out, and I have to say that was entirely my fault. We had purchased the two-story house in Oklahoma City together. This was the home in which we intended to live. Once the break up happened, I had to get her name off the mortgage. I was financially strapped and there were times I didn't know how I'd make it work.

I had to refinance the two-story house, which took everything I had. I was so strapped I had to pawn my favorite guitar (did I mention I'm a musician) and work on a reduced salary, as my company allowed me borrow money to keep my house. It was a tough time but I did it. I managed to fight through and make it work.

Now that the house was refinanced it was time to play catch up. I was still remodeling houses on the side and my Yukon house needed a lot of work. It was the middle of winter and I couldn't afford to get the heat turned on. It took four days for my new wall texture to dry because it was so cold in the house, and I really didn't know what I was doing.

I was working all the time and looking back I might have done some things differently. However, every time you face tough challenges, you're forced to fight your way through those experiences. It's what makes you who you are. Those hard times are the seeds of a better, smarter, stronger you. With that in mind, I don't think I'd change a thing.

My job was going well. I was working my rear end off and the owner was very happy with the job I was doing. I'll never forget how the owner of this company helped me when I was down. She gave me the kick I needed to get up and finish what I'd started. Sherri, I thank you to this day.

I worked my way up through the company and by the time I was 25, I was making $45,000 a year with a company car and three rental properties. I was able to pay off the loan from my employer. I spent the next year catching up from biting off more than I could chew.

By age 26 I'd capped out and reached my potential with the small company. I also bought another house at $25,000 and my EI was holding steady. I did have the opportunity to make bonuses, and I managed to earn every one of them, which increased my EI.

At 26, I was an account executive, thanks to egg rolls! I managed to sell a major distributor a very popular line of egg rolls. I no longer had a company car but a car allowance. Trust me; the company car is a much better deal. I had reached my income earning potential with this small company and was recruited for a position as a manufacturer representative, which requires a college degree. Being a manufacturer rep in the food service industry typically means a lot of travel. It's not uncommon to be out of town three to four days a week.

The reason I wanted to make the move to a manufacturer rep was that this job typically pays 50% more than I was making at the account executive level. I wanted that extra EI to feed my monster. I also wanted to be the quarterback with the large budget to take clients out to fancy dinners and great concerts. It happened, and it consumed my life. I became sidetracked for about 8 years and lost sight of what was important.

Landing a job with a great company and getting past the college degree requirement, because I already had five years of good experience in the industry, lends itself to a lesson. Don't let obstacles like "degree requirements" stop you from going for what you want.

Fortunately, the manufacturer rep position for which I was hired involved working only in the state of Oklahoma. Because the job didn't involve all the travel, it didn't pay the big bucks for which I was hoping. The new job did get me back into a company car with a $45,000 a year salary and bonus potential.

At 27, I got married and started a new job two weeks later. I quickly became the top sales rep in the country for this company. I had the advantage of already knowing my customers. I had to work my butt off to get that job, but with salary and bonus I made $72,000 in EI. My EI bubble had almost tripled in seven years.

In addition, I'd gained another income bubble through my beautiful wife's income. She has always been a hard worker and at the time worked four jobs and still does today. My wife was doing her regular job, dog sitting, bookkeeping, and also weekend work as an RN.

Let's take an inventory of my income bubbles at 27 years old.

Earned income of $72,000

Company car with free gasoline $10,000

Duplex $12,000

Yukon house $6,600

St. Clair house $6,000

Other jobs (mowing, home repair, etc) $2,000

Wife's income as an RN right out of college $45,000

As you can see, I had seven separate income bubbles at the age of 27. This made my total household income $153,600.

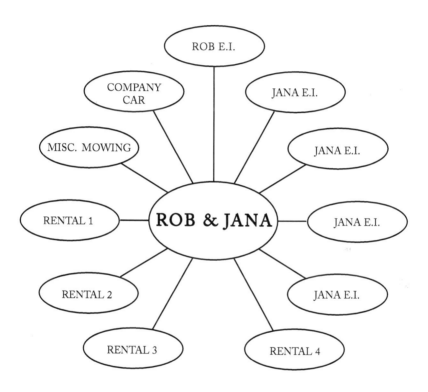

My wife had just received her associates RN degree and started out at $45,000 a year. She went on to get her bachelors later, but it didn't make any difference in pay.

We still lived in the same house that I purchased for $66,000 when I was 23 years old. We kept our expenses low and still do today. Keeping expenses low has always been a priority for us.

If you think of your living expenses from a business perspective, it makes sense to keep your overhead as low as possible. The lower your overhead, the more El you have to invest. Using your income to invest in creating new income bubbles is just good business.

I purchased another home in my hometown of Jones, Oklahoma. The opportunity presented itself to purchase the house right across from the high school. This was my chance to shout out to my small hometown, "Hey, I made it!"

I've now owned this little house for 13 years and the same people that originally rented it from me still live there. These people have been loyal and consistent and they've paid that house off for me. Now, that income bubble has increased because there's no debt against the property.

Each one of these properties produced a new income bubble for me. I'll get into detail about how to make that happen a little later. For now, I want to emphasize the power of multiple income streams. I'm sure you've heard the old saying, "Don't put all your eggs in one basket!" Multiple income streams or bubbles, allow you to diversify your risk.

In other words, if you have ten separate income streams of $300, you might lose one of those streams and it won't kill you. On the other hand, if you only have one income bubble like your job or EI and you lose that, you're devastated. That EI is necessary to provide shelter for your family and keep food on the table.

Over time, with a good plan and commitment, you can build additional income bubbles. Those additional income bubbles can eventually take the pressure off creating that EI. This was always my goal. Build my EI and invest as much of that as I could, so that someday, I wouldn't have to worry about a day job.

This can be a very realistic goal for most people. Still, too few have multiple income bubbles as a goal. I'm not going to tell you it's easy. That's the reason I'm giving you some of the details of my story. It wasn't easy. Sometimes it seemed impossible. Yet, today I can tell you without reservation, it was worth it!

We all have choices to make in life. We can choose to follow a proven path that will lead us to a better life in the future, or we can do what everyone else does. We can buy big homes, fancy new cars, and have all the toys, all the while digging ourselves into a pit of debt that we can't overcome.

You can follow my example and use the ideas in this book to build your own income bubbles. Even if you decide this business model isn't for you, invest in yourself. Create multiple income bubbles, allowing you to change your financial life.

THE YUPPIE YEARS
(DO AS I SAY, NOT AS I DID)

THIS CHAPTER IS ABOUT THINGS I DID THAT I don't recommend you do.

I allowed myself to get side tracked. I never lost sight of my goals, but I did lose focus of them. By losing focus, I slowed down the process of reaching my dream life.

This chapter is about how easy it is to lose your focus and the price that you'll pay for the lack of it.

Having grown up poor, it was easy to get sidetracked when I started seeing a lot of money coming in. I imagine this would be true for anyone, especially at such a young age. I had come out of poverty and worked my butt off six and seven days a week.

I was starting to really see the fruits of my labor. The cash flow was good and we were young and wanted to start enjoying our lives.

We started thinking about all the fun things we could buy with all this money we were making. In other words, we lost focus on building our assets and began focusing on spending our cash.

I think it's important that I talk about this because I think you need to be clear about what you're thinking. Always take time to step back and ask yourself some important questions; is this in the best interest of my goals, is doing _____ going to move me closer or farther away from where I want to be? I've learned the hard way, and you always need to be asking yourself these questions. I spent some time when I wasn't asking myself those questions. Because of that, I lost my focus of the goal.

I started going down a completely opposite path than the one that ultimately made me a millionaire. The good news is, I figured it out and made corrections to get back on the path to achieving my goals.

It started when my wife and I decided to buy a Land Cruiser. We loved that car and enjoyed every mile we put on it. We went into debt in order to enjoy that nice car.

We were now like many of our friends who drove new and expensive cars. When I look back on it now, I realize it wasn't such a bad thing to buy that car. We learned a valuable lesson from the experience, and as it turned out, that would be the last car payment we would ever make.

Buying the Land Cruiser was only the beginning. We were on a roll and determined to have the good things in life.

I'm not telling you not to have or want the nice things in life. What I'm suggesting is that you take a hard look at it before you sign on the dotted line. Ask yourself, "is this moving me closer or farther away from my goals?"

Next, we bought the lake house. When you own a lake house, you don't just have a lake house. You've got to have all the cool stuff that goes with a lake house, like golf carts to drive around. We had to have two golf carts, one for my wife and one for myself. You also have to have a boat. Why would you have a lake house and not have a boat? When you have a boat, you need some place to put it when you're not out on the lake. So we had to have a dock for the boat.

You may not realize this, but when it comes to boats, there are a lot of choices. I learned pretty fast that if I wanted to fish, I had to have a fishing boat. But if I wanted to cruise, the fishing boat wasn't going to cut, it.

This is where keeping up with the Jones' can cost you your fortune. You see, fishing out of a cruiser or cruising in a fishing boat isn't cool. This may be hard to believe, but there are people all over the lake that will help you understand how un-cool you are.

That's right; I had to have two boats. We had one boat for fishing and one boat for cruising and partying. Then, I had to have dock space for both boats.

Are you starting see where I'm going with all this? When you have a second home, you have two of everything plus the special toys that go with that home.

I had to have lawn mowers, weed eaters, blowers, and everything needed to take care of a home and a lawn. I had four wheelers and about anything else you could imagine you'd need with a lake house.

We also decided to remodel the lake house and add on a master bedroom and bath. So now in addition to all the other expenses of owning the lake house, we had building expenses too. We were living the high life.

This is where I tell you to do as I say and not as I did!

I spent eight years focusing on a non-income producing property. That property became a liability. Yes, we remodeled the house and it was beautiful when we were finished. Yes, we had all the toys, and yes we had a lot of fun going to the lake. We did enjoy our time with that lake house, but it did cost us.

It cost us money and more importantly, it cost us our focus. We stopped asking the key questions, and therefore stopped looking at our lives and our money like a business.

After eight years, my wife and I did a cost analysis on our expenses with the lake house. It was shocking to see that the average cost for a trip to the lake for us was $1500. I can tell you there were a lot of months during that time that we were at the lake two or three weekends out of the month.

Sometimes the only thing that makes sense is the numbers. Sometimes we don't want to look at the numbers because we already know what they're going to tell us.

The numbers are your friends, but only if you pay attention to them. They will let you know when you're starting down the wrong road. The numbers will tell you that you are moving away from your goals.

We continued to work hard and buy houses during the time that we had the lake house; we didn't actually quit doing what we were doing. But we did lose our focus, and that cost us money and time.

Had we not spent all that money and time focused on a non-income producing asset, I could have probably retired several years younger than I did.

The take away from this experience is that there will always be temptations and things and people that will try to distract you from your goals. It's your decision whether or not you allow those distractions to win.

If you want the nice things in life, and you should, understand the cost. In other words, make your plan and stick to it. If you want that new car, put it in your plan and work toward that goal. Just don't let the new car distract you from the real goal.

The real goal should be your long-term financial security. Building your wealth is the only way you'll ever really have true freedom. I'm talking about the kind of freedom to live your life on your terms instead of somebody else's terms.

Remember, if you're not following your plan, you're following someone else's!

TAXES, TAXES AND MORE TAXES!

IN THE LAST CHAPTER, I TALKED ABOUT my experience as a business owner. Now, it wasn't all bad. If you remember, I said running that business was the hardest thing I'd ever done. There's a lot that goes with business ownership today, especially if you have the type of business that has employees and a large overhead.

Part of that big overhead, that every business owner faces, is taxes. Everyone deals with taxes! We have to have taxes to support the infra structure of our nation. We pay taxes for schools, roads and bridges, police and fire protection, and the list goes on and on. I understand that we need a tax system to make things run.

However, the tax system we deal with today is far more than just supporting the needs that keep our country running. We are taxed every place we turn and for everything we do. We are taxed if we save money. We're taxed if we don't save money. We're even taxed if we die. I know I didn't pass the ACT and didn't go to some big college, but I'm not sure I'll ever be able to get my head around the concept of being taxed for dying.

As a business owner, I experienced a new level of taxation. Our system isn't set up to encourage entrepreneurship. It's almost as if it's designed to discourage capitalism and the entrepreneurial spirit that has made our country what it is. This chapter isn't about me complaining about our country or the way things work, though that may be what it sounds like right now.

The real purpose of this chapter is to tell you the story of what I experienced so that when that entrepreneurial spirit kicks in and you decide it's time to make your mark in the business world, you have your eyes wide open. You need to understand what you're up against and some of the challenges you'll face as an entrepreneur today.

I was a minority shareholder of a small to medium sized company. We were a contract sales agency. We represented food manufacturers from all over the world. We had a sales team of twelve people who made sales calls on hospitals, schools, restaurants, hotels, and any business that might sell prepared food to the public.

This company had a lot of entertainment expenses like college football tickets, NBA premium club level tickets, concert tickets, country club memberships, etc. Now that was great at first. I got the chance to attend some very cool events under the guise of entertaining clients and customers. It did get old over time. I spent a lot of time taking customers to events, and it took time away from my home life. This taught me the importance of time with family and friends.

Even though the company did very well, my EI remained around the $100,000 level. So my income wasn't any more than when I worked as a manufacturer's rep. Here is the kicker though. I had to file an individual tax return on the company's income, which put me over the $250,000 mark even though my salary was less than half that amount. What made it worse, that put me at a level where I couldn't take tax deductions on my fast growing real estate business.

I was paying so much in taxes, yet the tax code said the deductions would have to be deferred till my adjusted gross income fell below the $250,000 level. This means that any plumber, contractor or employee I hired was a nondeductible expense. It meant that I was working eight days a week patching sheet rock, mowing lawns, etc. because Uncle Sam was punishing me for working hard. The harder I worked, the more money I made, the more people I employed, the more taxes I owed.

Now, that all sounds like a good reason to give up and just go back to getting by with an eight to five job. I don't want to give you the impression that it's so bad you can't get over the hump. You can get over the hump. You just have to take the time to plan your business.

For me it was motivation to get my ducks in a row. I needed to get out from owning a profitable company that only paid me $100,000 a year for owning it. The math didn't add up. After owning the company for five years and not being able to take deductions, I had over half a million dollars in deferred tax deductions. Yet, I'm only able to take $25,000 a year of those deferred deductions. Which are how many years of deductions? 20 freakin' years are you kidding me?

So when you hear someone claim the rich don't pay taxes, they don't have a clue what they're talking about. The only way to start declaring deductions was to call myself a real estate professional. So, according to the IRS that's what I am. I'm really a maintenance man, a Millionaire Maintenance Man.

The thing that people don't seem to understand is this, if I didn't pay so much in taxes, I'd be able to hire more people.

It doesn't matter if you make $30,000 a year or a $100,000 a year, your still going to be taxed 25% on your profits. Let's say that you sell a house and make $100,000 profit. You're going to have to pay 25% plus on your profits. Then that $100,000 will be added to your adjusted gross household income. So now you get to pay the capital gains taxes on that same $100,000 profit from the sale of that house. But keep in mind, capital gains is taxed at a slightly lower rate than EI.

This is why I say that your best bet for wealth building is long term rental property investment. Maybe you've seen the shows on television about flipping houses instead of renting or long term investing. The show will have five, good looking guys or an attractive husband and wife team that spend eight weeks getting a house ready to flip. Then they'll clear anywhere from $50,000 to $150,000, sometimes less.

Let's take a look at that again. After real estate fees and capital gains taxes plus EI taxes, there's not that much money to split between five or six people. The only way to make that work is to have several projects going at the same time, which would be very hard to manage.

I've thought about this a lot over the years, and I can't make the numbers add up. Flipping houses can generate good revenue. I don't doubt that at all. However, when you factor in the tax liability, you wind up making very little clear profit on a big investment. I see the risk/reward ratio of that business model as too risky for long-term wealth building.

I know there are lots of people that are out there buying and flipping homes. I don't doubt that they are able to make some good money in the process. However, when you factor in the taxes, it makes more sense to invest in real estate as a long-term investment. By focusing on creating positive cash flow from each property, you build your asset base plus your income without the tax burden that comes with flipping.

Taxes are a part of our life today. It's part of living in our country. I want you to understand that it's important to have good and reliable tax advice before you get too deep into your business. Taxes can be handled and planned for if you have the right tax advice to help you navigate the complexities of our ever-changing tax system. The law this year will be something completely different next year.

If you're a business owner, you don't have time to learn everything about the tax code and how to best navigate it. You have to be focused on doing whatever drives revenue for your business. Make sure you have a tax professional on your team that can help you stay ahead of the wolf that is our tax system.

We'll talk more about building your team a little

later in the book. For now, it's important that you keep in mind that a good tax pro on your team will not only save you some headaches, but they'll actually make you money.

MILLIONAIRE THINKING 101

IN THIS CHAPTER WE'RE GOING TO DISCUSS the thinking that goes with becoming a millionaire. Even if becoming a millionaire isn't your goal in life, the thought processes that make millionaires is key to success in any endeavor. It's important to start thinking like successful people think.

You may be thinking to yourself, "Why do I need to read this?" To answer that question, let me ask you a question, "Do you know anyone that is highly successful?" Maybe you personally know a self-made millionaire. If you do, you may have already noticed the way they think might be different than the way you think. Maybe you've had discussions in the past and noticed a different attitude about many of the basics in life.

You may have noticed they think differently about consumer debt. They think differently about spending rather than investing. They think differently about the day-to-day challenges we all face. They react differently to outside forces. They don't have time to indulge in complaining and criticizing. They are more interested in ideas that will help them become more efficient while trying to reach their goals.

Millionaires think differently than 95% of the population. That's the reason they're millionaires. I've heard people say things like, "If I had his money I'd be able to do what he does." Everybody wants to spend a million dollars, but not everyone wants to work for a million dollars! Maybe you've had the same thought run through your mind. If you have, you're not alone. This is the way the majority of people think. This is the difference between those that create wealth and the rest of us. That mindset that says, "I need money to make money," is killing your ability to build wealth and success in your life.

I know that you're wondering how this is going to tie into investing in single-family homes and renting them to build long-term wealth. That's a fair question and here's the answer...your thinking is everything! When it comes to being successful and building wealth, your thinking shapes your attitudes about you, your money, and the way you spend and invest. Your thinking determines how you view yourself and the world around you.

So, if you're not living the life that you think you should be living, it's because of the way you think. The good news is you can change that. You can model the successful mindset of a millionaire, and if you do, you'll start to experience positive results for your efforts.

I'm not going to give you a bunch of motivational concepts and ideas. I'm not here to walk you through ways you can change your thinking. I'm not here to tell you how to clear the limiting beliefs that have held you back. There are plenty of resources available that can help you with those challenges. I do believe that if you're not living the life that you feel you should be living; you owe it to yourself and the people you love to find out the reason. Invest in yourself and figure out what's holding you back so you can fix it and move forward with your life and your success.

This brings me to the first idea that separates the average from the wealthy. The wealthy believe that they are in complete control of their destiny. They take full responsibility for their lives. They take responsibility for their successes and their failures. They don't blame the economy, the government, their parents, or anything else that is outside of their control. They understand that we all have circumstances, but they don't let circumstances become excuses.

I know we are all dealing with a lot of stuff every day. We have the kids, the job, the bills, and everything that goes with everyday life. It's easy to let that become all-consuming and keep us from doing the things that can make the biggest difference. It's easy to become overwhelmed with all that we have on our plates. We will often use all the noise in our lives as excuses for not taking action. I'm talking about the kind of action that can change your life. I'm talking about doing that one thing every day that will make you wealthy down the road. I'm also talking about reading that one book that can have a dramatic impact on your life.

Don't let the excuse of being too busy prevent you from changing the way you live. Look at the successful people you know and observe the way they think. Watch the way they deal with circumstances. I promise, you'll see that they handle the everyday turmoil of life differently than most people do.

The big idea here is to understand that they are successful because of the way they think. They don't think the way they do because they're successful. Success and wealth happens in the mind first. When you can start to think like a successful person, you'll start to act like a successful person, and this is where it all begins.

So drop the excuses! If you are complaining about something or making excuses about something, you can change. Instead of wasting your time and energy complaining about the economy, the government, or

MILLIONAIRE MAINTENANCE MAN

your boss, figure out how to make it better, and take action. Millionaires don't waste time complaining and criticizing. Millionaires look at problems as potential opportunities, and they take action. Where others see roadblocks, successful people see an opening for improvement. They see an opportunity to make things better. Instead of wasting time and energy complaining, they look for a way to change what's not efficient and improve it.

The 95% spend all their time complaining and looking for someone else to solve the problem. They don't believe they are capable of making changes. They think that they are the victims of circumstance. They allow the speed bumps of life to knock them off course, and then blame their failure on outside influences.

The successful have outside influences and circumstances, too. They have obstacles that must be overcome in order to achieve their goals. Instead of complaining and wasting time and energy looking outside for the answers, they look inside and take full responsibility for everything in their lives.

We all have circumstances. We all have to deal with the government, the IRS, the economy, and all of the other outside influences that make up our world. The difference is in the way we deal with those circumstances. If you let all the outside influences determine whether or not you take action on your goals, you'll never take action. If you wait for the timing to be perfect, you'll never get started. If you wait for everything to be just right, it'll never happen.

To be wealthy, you have to learn to think like the wealthy. If you want things to change in your life, you have to change, and that change has to start with the way you think. So, I challenge you to look at your own thinking. Observe the thoughts you have every day. Be the watcher of your mind. If you are constantly thinking and saying things that are counter-productive to you achieving the life you want, question those thoughts. You may not even be aware of the thoughts you have. Take time to look at what's happening in your mind. If it doesn't serve you, change your thinking.

I also challenge you to learn how the rich think. I'm not talking about the heir to a fortune. I'm talking about the self-made entrepreneur that has created an amazing life. Look for successful people you already know, watch how they think and act, and model them. You owe it to yourself to examine what you're doing. If it's not working, change it.

If it is working but not the way you hoped, look for inspiration from others and tweak what you're doing so you can accelerate your results. We can all improve and it's our duty to make the effort.

The bottom line is, you're reading this book because something about the idea of building a better financial future appeals to you. Somewhere inside you is the entrepreneur that wants more than what the 8 to 5 can give. You want to improve your finances, and by doing so, improve your life. Well, the good news is, you're on the right track. You can do anything you want in life if you're willing to learn.

HOW TO THINK
FOR LONG-TERM WEALTH

IN THIS CHAPTER I WANT TO GO A LITTLE deeper into the thinking that has allowed many people, including myself, to achieve wealth that will last decades, possibly generations.

In the previous chapter we talked about, the way you think directly affecting the way you handle every part of your life. Your thinking affects your relationships, your money, your happiness, and your overall view of the world in which you live. I submit that if you're not happy with your life as it is today, it's time to examine the way you think.

For this chapter we'll assume you're not living your dream life. You may have a job you don't like anymore, or you may like your job but you don't make enough money. Whatever your situation, it can change, and that change starts with the way you think.

If you know someone that has achieved a level of success that you admire, take a hard look at their attitudes and the way they think. Don't be afraid to approach these people. Everyone loves flattery. Look for a first generation millionaire. Look at everything they do and ask why they do it that way. Learn why they think the way they do. Then use that as contrast. Compare your thinking to theirs and notice the differences. I'll bet if you really do this exercise, you'll come up with some serious differences in how they think about many aspects of life and business.

When I talk about success here, I'm not just talking about income. It's not really the income that matters. It's more about what you do with the money you make. We can probably all come up with examples of people that made fortunes while starting out with a small income. Yet, their thinking is what led them to handle their money in a way that yielded big returns over time. It wasn't luck or being in the right place at the right time. It was the way they thought about and handled the money they did make.

I'll give you some examples of what I'm talking about. At the age of 35, I had a household income of $260,000 a year. That's pretty good money by anyone's standards, right? At 35 with that kind of income, we still lived in the same house I paid $66,000 for when I was 23.

Too many people with household incomes of $250,000 a year get tied down with liability type assets like a $500,000 home and a BMW. It's too common to see young couples with families that are deep in debt. They look like they're living the perfect life of abundance on the outside. Yet, in far too many cases, these people are living paycheck to paycheck. They've let themselves become slaves to the luxuries they worked so hard to obtain.

On the other hand, I chose to live a more moderate lifestyle and invest that "big house and fancy car" money into as many small income bubbles as my time would allow. My chosen method of investment is real estate. My wife and I made a conscious decision to keep our lifestyle at or below our means so we could invest in our futures and ourselves.

I also invested in myself by using my assets to purchase stock in a company I co-owned. So, whether I'm investing in a business or real estate, I'm investing my assets rather than tying them up in consumer debt. That consumer debt is the downfall of so many people today. I can't tell you how many people I know that have over purchased a home and now that home owns them. They spend all their time and energy trying to keep up so the sharks don't take it all away.

I've often asked my good friends living that lifestyle, "What would happen if you lost your jobs?" Most people have it in their minds that they can go find another job tomorrow paying the same income and benefits. Unfortunately, life doesn't work that way. In today's economy, companies can have layoffs and hard times. Even the wealthiest of companies go through cut backs and downsizing.

Because of this, you can't afford to spend all the money you make. I've seen some very talented people lose their high paying positions and it cost them everything. Companies have to make a profit in order to stay in business. Hard times and slow sales will force a company to look at cost cutting measures in order to stay in business.

Every business is running leaner today than they were even a few short years ago. If you're working for a company, be aware that there is no guarantee. You're expendable, if that's what it takes to keep the company in business.

I don't understand why so many people are against capitalism. The nuts and bolts of a business are its employees. Employees want a raise every year. However, the employer's general costs, taxes, and insurance costs go up every year, just as the cost of living goes up for the employees. So, the decision on whether to give raises or keep everyone employed carries a heavy load. Employees must consider all the costs involved with running a company that provides jobs.

Companies are faced with increasing costs for unemployment, insurance and payroll taxes, not to mention corporate taxes. All the taxes are what make the cost of doing business in this country the highest in the world.

With that in mind, how does one expect employers to maintain the increasing cost of doing business? Once again, if you have a job, you should thank your employer. You're fortunate to have that job and you need to appreciate your employer for allowing you to work there. They've given you a gift, and you really shouldn't take that gift for granted. That job, that you may not like, is providing you with EI. When was the last time your boss got a raise?

You have the right and the opportunity to use that EI to invest in yourself and your future. None of which would be possible without that company for which you are working. I always wonder from where the anti-capitalist is coming. Do they really understand what it takes to run a successful business in this day and age? I somehow doubt it.

You have a job, and you are producing an income. Are you spending all your income on consumer goods?

Have you made some mistakes along the way and are ready to change? There will never be a better time than right now to commit to making whatever changes need to be made to give yourself the capital to invest in your future.

Figure out how to get out of debt. Down size and free up your capital so that you can save and invest in your future. Do it for yourself and for your family. I'm sure you've heard the old phrase, "A penny saved is a penny earned." If that's true, you have to ask yourself how many pennies are you saving?

If you're not saving, you're not really earning. Think about that for a minute! If you're spending everything you make, you have no assets to invest. You can change that, and you need to if you're going to create long-term wealth.

If I were to go back to my younger days, my Robin Hood dream would have been something like this: We wouldn't have spent the money to buy a house or pay off a car or anything else that's responsible. We'd spend it all on fancy vacations, clothes, new fancy cars, and big homes. All that would have sounded wonderful at the time but the reality is, twenty years later we would've been in worse shape than we were then. We'd be living up all our income and have little to show for it. What we have would really belong to the bank or credit card companies. In reality, we wouldn't have owned anything. All our fancy stuff would have owned us.

There's a reason people are poor! They lack what I call financial intelligence or the discipline to use their financial intelligence. I'm a millionaire! That doesn't mean I have a million dollars in the bank. I have a massive portfolio of income producing rental properties that would be worth well over a million dollars if I were to sell them. I don't sell them because the taxes would be way too high.

I drive a 2000 GMC pickup truck. It's paid for and I carry liability insurance only. My wife drives a 2005 Honda hybrid that gets 42 miles to the gallon and it's also paid for with liability insurance. We take the Honda if we go on a long distance trip. Everything my wife purchases is with a coupon. She only shops at thrift stores for her clothing. She's never had any credit card debt or any debt at all that I'm aware of in the 20 years we've been together.

Don't get me wrong my wife loves to shop. When she goes shopping, she'll come home with several outfits that look like department store stuff, yet she only paid $30 for all of it. She shops the thrift stores and always uses coupons when she can. She is thrifty with her money and is responsible for teaching me financial intelligence.

She makes good money and doesn't need my money at all. We keep separate bank accounts and handle our own money. This is the way her parents did it and it's worked well for us. I've borrowed money from her in the past and she has borrowed money from me. It really doesn't matter that it gets paid back, but it always does.

The point I want to emphasize here, even though we make a lot of money and have the financial means to do a lot of things, the important thing to us is living comfortable lives and building our future wealth. We don't need or want bigger more expensive houses, fancy high dollar cars, or any of those things. We live comfortably in a very nice, older home and take great vacations every year. We do all the things most people do or want to do. The difference is that we do it all without creating consumer debt.

We don't borrow money for lifestyle. We only borrow money to invest in new income bubbles. We both work hard, and we both love what we do. That's really the key to the whole thing. I love buying old houses, and making them beautiful. My wife loves what she does, and together we're very happy. We work our butts off, and we love it. As the old saying goes, "If you love what you do, you'll never work a day in your life." That's exactly how my wife and I live our lives. We take two nice vacations each year. We live very comfortably in a nice home. We go out if we want to, and we get our share of TV watching. I like to play my guitar and drink my beer, too. I don't drink before five PM because I like beer more than I should. I do have rules set for myself. I take care of my business first.

I still work part time for the company in which I used to be part owner. They need me now and then, and it helps break up the monotony of constantly remodeling houses. I do it because I still enjoy it, and it's another income bubble for me.

So let me ask you some questions. If you were a millionaire, what kind of house would you buy? What kind of car would you drive? Would you buy a boat and a lake house? Do you have the experience to control that kind of capital? What kind of financial intelligence do you have? Would I let you run my company? Would you let you run a company? How many lottery winners and professional athletes have we seen go broke because of lack of financial intelligence?

These are all important questions that you need to ask yourself. Then pay very close attention to your answers. Even if you're not currently running a company or you're not a millionaire, you need to think about this. Your life is a business. If you run your personal life like a business, like a millionaire would run his or her business, you'll soon find yourself out of debt. If you learn to think like a millionaire, you'll soon have the extra capital to invest in yourself. You'll soon be able to change your financial life. If you can learn to think like

I've discussed in these last two chapters, you'll be well on your way to being wealthy.

Remember, wealthy people who are self-made, don't think like they do because they have a lot of money. They have a lot of money because they think like they do.

SECTION 3

TIME TO GET BUSY

SO FAR WE'VE TALKED ABOUT HOW I STARTED with nothing and retired at the age of forty. We've talked about my poor upbringing and how that caused me to decide that I'd never live like that again. We've gone into detail about my story and I think it's important. I want you to know that no matter where you come from, no matter what your circumstance, you can succeed.

We've talked about work ethic. It's important to have a solid work ethic because you'll never make it in business without work ethic. Your determination and work ethic are the two assets you can count on to see you through. That's why it's important to talk about them. Sometimes it's all a person has to start with. It's certainly all I had when I started. As it turned out, it was good enough. Sure it would've been a little easier if I'd had some money. I may have been able to get where I am faster. But, I managed with hard work and determination to accomplish by forty, what many don't accomplish in a lifetime.

We also talked about traditional business ownership and some of the challenges that go with it. It's the hardest thing I've ever done, and I found out first hand that it wasn't for me. The work was hard and in order to be successful, I had to eat, sleep and breathe that business. I learned I didn't own the business, it owned me. Sure there were a lot of good things that came out of it. The lessons I learned are priceless. The experience made me a better boss and businessman. Most of all the experience made me more determined than ever to build my own business my way.

We've touched on taxes and the costs of doing business in our world. The costs of doing business continue to rise and the bureaucracy continues to make keeping the doors open more difficult. There are payroll taxes, income taxes, corporate taxes, and taxes on inventory. You name it, and they will tax it.

Finally, we talked about the mindset of wealth. The millionaire mindset is the most important topic to be discussed yet. If you don't have the financial intelligence to use your money wisely, it won't matter how much money you make. You'll always be in a bind. You'll always be under pressure to make more because you weren't able to manage what you had. We talked about the value of learning from a mentor or at least a role model. Observe the way the wealthy think, and learn to think like they do and to achieve similar results.

Now you're ready. You have everything you need to start building your wealth. You have all the basic knowledge so you can start taking action and change your financial future one investment at a time.

BECOMING A MILLIONAIRE ONE HOUSE AT A TIME

—▬▬◀ ▶▬▬

WE'VE BEEN TALKING ABOUT THE MILLIONAIRE mindset and how that kind of thinking can and will change your financial life. If you're following along, you're working on getting out of debt. You have to free up your assets and income so you have money to invest.

Get rid of consumer debt as fast as you can, without ruining your credit. If you live in a home that's more than you need, sell it. Get rid of the new car, and buy a car that doesn't require a payment. Your first step in building wealth is to get rid of consumer debt.

Wealthy people think differently than the everyday working man or woman. They think in terms of cash flow and tax liability. They ask themselves questions like "Can I write off this expense?"

Learning to think like a millionaire isn't that hard to do. There are plenty of tools and books available today that will help you start thinking and acting in a way that will ultimately improve your financial life. A good place to start would be some of Dave Ramsey's books. He gives step-by-step instructions on how to completely reshape your financial life. After you read Dave Ramsey's books to learn how to get out of debt, I would like to recommend some of my favorite wealth building books, which are: The Richest Man in Babylon by George S. Clason, Rich Dad Poor Dad by Robert T. Kiyosaki, and The Millionaire Next Door by Thomas J. Stanley.

Getting out of debt is the first step to becoming wealthy. I'm talking about consumer debt for things that are never going to make you money. Reduce your lifestyle expenditures. I used to just shake my head when I saw employees coming in with Starbucks coffee every morning. We had all the coffee anyone could drink at the office, but they paid for expensive coffee every day of the week. Think about the long-term cost of that. Five days a week at five dollars a cup adds up to $1300 a year. That's the kind of expense I'm suggesting that you eliminate, and use that money to create additional income bubbles for yourself.

Find other ways to free up your cash. Maybe you have a newer car with a payment. Think about selling that car and buying an older car that you can own without a payment. You don't need to keep up with the

Jones'. They're not going to pay your bills or contribute to your retirement. So why even consider trying to keep up with them. Instead, shut down your spending, and use that money to buy income-producing properties. If you do, in a few short years, the Jones' will be stressed out trying to keep up with you.

There are all kinds of ways to generate additional income and to cut expenses. Take a look around your house. Are there clothes in the closets you don't wear? Sell them on eBay. Is there stuff you don't use or need anymore? Run a Craigslist add. Take a second job. Do what you have to do right now so that later you can do what you want. I know some of this may sound a little over the top, and that's okay. It won't be too over the top in a few years when you have thousands of dollars a month in passive income.

I look at second jobs as a good thing. My wife works four jobs. I don't care what you do, but you do have to take action. Do whatever it takes because if you keep doing what you're doing, nothing will change. Figure out ways to increase your available cash and get busy. Don't worry about spending money on your hobbies right now. Make your income producing properties your hobby. You'll have plenty time later to have all the hobbies you want because you won't be tied down to a job.

Look at it like this, you go to work every day and you expect a raise each year because your cost of living keeps going up. I'm suggesting that you create your own raise. I'm actually suggesting that you create two raises, one from reducing your cost of living and the other from creating additional income bubbles that will grow over the years. This month I gave myself a $12,000 a year raise. Now, I had to work for that raise but it is worth it.

You're asking, how did you give yourself a $12,000 raise? I had to remodel two houses after the tenants either purchased a home or moved out of state. One of those tenants has been with me for over ten years. He was a great tenant and I rarely raised his rent over that ten years. Now that he's moved on, it's time to collect. I remodeled the house, raised the rent, and then leased it again. It happens, and it can happen for you, but you have to get yourself ready.

Now that you're out of debt, let's go make that first investment. You'll need money to get started. Take out a second mortgage on your home; use the money you're saving after getting out of consumer debt. Find some money so you can get your first investment property and start building your financial future. This is how you can go from an everyday working stiff to a millionaire entrepreneur the Jones' will envy.

If you're established and have some savings and good credit, you're primed and ready to take action. If however, you're just getting started you'll want to become an owner occupant for every house you purchase.

Remember my first house was a small duplex with one side rented. I purchased that property as an owner occupant to keep my initial costs as low as possible. Keep in mind that I had a company car and no other expenses when I bought that duplex. I lived in one side while the other side paid most of the mortgage. I was making $22,000 a year at the time but I made it work. A few years later I cashed out my 401K to pay off that property.

Two years later I bought the $66,000 house. I bought both of those houses as an owner occupant so my interest rates were better than a typical investment type conventional loan. I lived in that $66,000 dollar house most of my adult life. That means that I had to put 20-25% down for a conventional loan on each additional investment property. What I'm saying is; that if you can buy your properties as an owner occupant... that is the cheapest way to go!

I kept buying houses, fixing them up, and leasing them. That's the reason I'm no longer working in the corporate world. I did it one house at a time, and that's what I'm suggesting you do. Make that first investment and start generating positive cash flow. Then rinse and repeat.

Positive cash flow is the key. You have to work for positive cash flow on each property you purchase. Even when that cash flow is only a few hundred dollars, it adds up as you add properties to your portfolio. Imagine if you had ten properties pay you positive cash flow of three hundred dollars a month each. What would that do for your stress level?

How would you feel to know that you had an additional $3,000 coming in the first of each month? Would you sleep better at night? Would you take your family on that vacation of your dreams? Or would you take that cash flow and invest in more income producing properties? This takes us right back to the kind of thinking that makes millionaires. You can choose that vacation, new car, or some toy if you want. However, the millionaire mindset would have you investing your profits in more income producing properties.

Think about how it will feel to have 10, 15, 20 or more income bubbles from positive cash flow properties each month. Close your eyes and feel it. Imagine it and see the rent checks filling your mailbox. Imagine filling out both sides of your deposit slip and needing to use another.

This is a perfect business model for anyone, especially if you're young and just getting started in your financial life. You haven't had time to run up a lot of consumer debt and get yourself in a financial mess. However, don't discount this business even if you are older.

It doesn't matter if you're 20 years old or 50. You can make this model work for you to create positive cash flow. Just because you've been around a while doesn't mean you're too old to get yourself moving. Age doesn't matter. You can do this and change your financial life. So stop standing in quick sand and get moving!

For example, I have a nephew that is 25 years old. He works a full time job paying $35,000 a year and has completed some college.

His entrepreneur mindset is serving him well and will continue to serve him throughout his life. I've been coaching him, not babysitting him. He lives in another state. The lessons we've learned together is to keep expenses low and invest to create positive cash flow, and he's learned this lesson well. Currently, while writing this book, my 25 year old nephew owns 12 income producing properties and continues to work his EI job. That is 13 income producing bubbles.

I'm all about getting a good education. However, he's already earned his degree in my opinion. He's figured out that the most important education you can get is generating positive cash flow and handling your money. He's kicking my ass in income bubbles when I was his age and I'm so proud of him!

I tell you the story of my nephew to emphasize that it doesn't matter where you are or how much money you make right now, you can make small changes and completely reverse your financial future. If you're young and just starting out, like my other nephew who is 19, you're off to a great start. If you're older you may have a different advantage.

You may already have some savings and established credit that you can use to create income bubbles instead of consumer debt. The only thing holding you back is your own thinking. If you read this and question your ability to make this work, go back and take a look at your thinking. Compare your thinking to that self-made millionaire that you know. Ask them questions and get into their head. Your time is now, and your opportunity is right in front of you.

Now you can see and feel what it's like to have that cash flow coming in each month. Let's take a closer look at the magic of positive cash flow and how to create it, one house at a time.

POSITIVE CASHFLOW IS KING

POSITIVE CASH FLOW IS THE LIFEBLOOD of any business. It is, in fact, the key to financial freedom whether you are in business or working for someone else. You must create positive cash flow to save, invest, and grow your income and business. With everything you do and every penny you spend, creating positive cash flow should be the number one consideration.

Look at life without positive cash flow. Maybe you're living in that kind of circumstance now. If you're living in negative cash flow, there is good news. You can change it. You can change your life and live in positive cash flow.

Here's the not so good news! You won't be able to go from negative cash flow to positive cash flow by doing the same things you've done in the past. You'll have to handle your money differently. I know it can be overwhelming and seem difficult, but it's worth the effort.

Everything I've done in my adult life has been designed to create positive cash flow. I worked hard in the corporate world to grow my EI. I lived below my means, keeping my living expenses low. I drove company cars. When the company cars went away, I chose to drive an older vehicle so I didn't have payments and could carry liability insurance only.

I worked my main job and then mowed yards on the side to generate additional income. My wife works four jobs to this day in order to keep the cash flow high while our expenses remain low. We choose to live like this because we understand that positive cash flow is king.

Living with a positive cash flow mindset may sound painful. It may sound like we suffer and don't get or do the good things in life. I'm here to tell you that the reality is the opposite. Because we plan our life to create and grow our positive cash flow, we are free. We're free to go and do anything we want. We take nice vacations each year and enjoy our lives each day. We choose to live the way we do because it allows us the freedom of choice.

Consider the consequences of living your life in a negative cash flow life style. First, you can only operate on negative cash flow for so long. Eventually, the inevitable happens, and it all comes crashing down around you.

Maybe you're not in negative cash flow. Maybe you have been in the past or are currently just barely getting by. Think about the amount of stress that situation creates in your life. Most of us have experienced the pain of wondering where the money is going to come from to pay the bills.

Some people spend most of their lives living under that kind of pressure. I bet if you've ever experienced that feeling of lack, that feeling of wondering where the money is going to come from, you didn't like it. I'm willing to bet that if you're in that position now, you'd love to change it.

Maybe you're upside down and have negative cash flow, or maybe you are just breaking even. In either case, you are placing yourself under unnecessary stress. Wouldn't it be better to cut back the lifestyle expenses and free yourself from the stress and worry that keeps you awake at night?

Ask yourself, "What's the price I'm paying now to live the way I live?" If you're stressed about money or the lack of it, you need to take a look at your thinking and evaluate your priorities when it comes to your spending and lifestyle.

I don't have the stress of wondering where the money is going to come from to pay the bills. I don't think about it because I don't have consumer debt. I don't live above my means, and I don't care what the guy next door drives to work.

I know that I have the money in the bank and the consistent cash flow to support my lifestyle. If I want to take a vacation, the money is there. If I want to buy a different car, the money is there. The difference is that I don't want that new car. It's not part of my vision for my future. I'd rather do without that new car and take that money and invest in more income producing properties to increase my cash flow.

I deal with none of that stress we talked about. I can't imagine making the choice to lie awake at night because I've got more month than money. I don't need that kind of stress and don't understand why people choose to live that way. It is a choice, you know.

I understand that we get caught up in what society teaches us. We somehow think we need to live up to the standards of others. Yet, when we look at that concept and think with a rational mind, we realize that none of those people who criticize are going to pay our bills or contribute to our retirement. That being the case, doesn't it make more sense to cut back your expenses so that you can live with a positive cash flow?

It may not be easy to change the way you think, but if you're in the situation I described above, it's important that you do change your thinking. Money is a tool. It's a tool that can be used for good or bad. It doesn't have feelings or a soul. It comes into your life and flows back out of your life. That's what money is designed to do, flow in and out of your life. That means that you have the choice of how you handle your money. You can choose to spend it all on the next shiny thing, or you can choose to save some and invest some so in the future you will have a stress free life.

I've created my life so my cash flow continues to increase whether I buy more properties or not. I've been doing this now for twenty years. Over those twenty years, many of the properties have been paid off. That means I no longer have mortgages on those properties. I bought property, invested money and sweat, and then I leased the property for a positive cash flow. Even if that cash flow was only $200 a month it was positive.

Over the years, tenants come and go. Their circumstances change. They transfer to a new location or they buy their own home. Whatever the reason, when they move, I will update the home and lease it again for a higher rent. Boom! My cash flow just went up. In addition to that, the people that are renting the house are essentially paying off the mortgage for me. When that mortgage is paid off, I then have a giant increase in cash flow from that property.

I want you to really get the big picture here. It's not about the investment per say. It's about the positive cash flow you can generate from that investment.

To make a point, I'd like for you to do a little visualization here. Imagine for a moment that you have ten properties. All ten properties are leased and you are earning $200 a month in positive cash flow from each for a total of $2000 a month. That's not too shabby is it? As good as that might sound, it gets better over time.

$24,000 per year

Now let's say that each of those properties have permanent financing for ten years. The mortgages on each are $600 a month. So as each property pays off, you gain an extra $600 a month in positive cash flow. This is just an example, to make a point, so we're keeping the numbers simple here.

You started off with ten homes paying you $2000 a month or $24,000 a year. Over time, the mortgages on the properties pay off. For each mortgage that pays off, you get a raise of $600 a month or an additional $7200 a year. When all ten properties are mortgage free, you would have positive cash flow of $72,000 a year plus the $24,000 a year you were already earning in positive cash flow from rents. That's a nice passive income of $96,000 a year, which is far less taxed than EI.

$96,000 per year

Sure there are things that will change the numbers like increasing property taxes and insurance premiums. You'll have maintenance costs and so on. However, you'll also have increasing rents over the course of time.

I try not to raise the rent on my properties until a tenant moves out and lease it to someone else. I operate this way because I'm a people person, and I think it pays me well to take good care of my customers (tenants). However, sometimes the property taxes and insurance costs will force a raise in rent. I don't get into a negative cash flow on a property. So if costs go up to the point that my cash flow is break even or negative, I'm forced to raise the rent. However, that rarely happens.

I also believe this is one of the reasons that I don't have much turn over with my tenants. They rent from me and stay with me a long time because I take good care of them. I treat them like what they are, my customers.

We'll talk more about the way I handle my customers in a later chapter. For now I want you to get your teeth into the idea that positive cash flow is the ultimate goal.

Whether you're buying income producing properties or working for someone else, you have to generate positive cash flow because it's the lifeblood of your financial life, both present and future.

THE NUTS, BOLTS AND PAINTBRUSHES

LET'S TALK ABOUT THE PROCESS OF DOING the remodel. This is the biggest step in the process after you've purchased the property. Before we get too deep into the remodel let's cover some of the basics.

I like older homes for investment properties. I prefer homes built in the 1920's and 30's. I live in a historical district of Oklahoma City where most all of the homes fall into this timeline. It's a perfect scenario for me, as a majority of my rental properties are within a two-mile radius of my home. This allows me to be on-site often. I get to see what's going on with the properties and catch little maintenance issues before they become big issues.

The Law of Attraction has taken over, and my last ten houses have found me. Because I have taken the time to form relationships with my tenants/customers, they will let me know if a friend or family member needs to sell a house because of a hardship or simply a life change. They will let me know if a friend or family needs a place to live.

I like these older homes because of the way they were constructed. I like that they have a good bone structure. In other words, they are sound, as far as the basic construction goes. I can give the outside a nice facelift and remodel the inside. Once that is done, I have a home that's beautiful and that will produce a nice rental income. I'm always looking for opportunities to pick up properties that are reasonably close to me. I'm also looking for properties that need work.

I do all of the remodel work except for the three "Bigs," electricity, plumbing, and heat and air. These tasks need to be done by a licensed professional with millions in insurance in case anything was to ever happen. I have learned to do most of this stuff over the years and I enjoy it. It gives me a good feeling to go in and convert an older house from an eye sore to a beauty. I learned how to do this stuff by trial and error and YouTube. You can learn how to do anything these days by watching YouTube videos.

This is a sweat equity business. You make your money, not by paying contractors for services, but by doing things yourself. It's important that you understand this from the start. If you're willing to get a little dirty and spend some time with a paintbrush, you can build yourself a business that will create good cash flow and over time, create a lot of wealth.

Finding properties that need work is a key to my business model. You can't pay the price of a newly remodeled home and still generate positive cash flow from rent. Well, maybe you can but it's going to be more difficult to do and I like easy. I like to know that when I purchase a property I can transform it from old and ugly into modern and beautiful. This is how I buy properties at a lower price.

Once I make that property beautiful, I can charge premium rent for the property. I also help increase the value of not just my property but also the other properties around it. I've even seen neighbors suddenly take an interest in upgrading their homes. It just seems to catch on and the entire neighborhood improves.

Once I find the property and get it purchased, it's time to go to work. I recommend that you always start on the inside of the house first. Get the inside part of the project completed as fast as possible so you can rent the property. You can always work on the outside after the home is rented. You just need to make sure you are prompt with your work so you don't inconvenience your tenant. Remember that your tenant is your customer so treat them with respect and courtesy, and they'll be your customer for a long time.

Now let's talk about the actual work that goes into the remodel. When you watch HGTV or Flip This House you'll notice that these people are always going to the most expensive places to buy their materials. It seems there is always a wife that wants to shop in the specialty shops and expensive show rooms. I cringe when I look at the cost they have in some of their remodels.

I get the bulk of my materials at Lowe's and Home Depot. You can get one of their 5% credit cards to help with additional savings on your materials and they have just about everything you will need to make your homes beautiful. The other advantage for me is that I have both stores within four miles of where I live, so time wasted commuting back and forth is cut to a minimum.

Since most of my homes are from the 20's and 30's they all have beautiful oak hardwood floors. These beautiful floors may be covered up with carpet or something else, but they are there. I love hardwood and so do most renters. Carpet is nasty and would have to be replaced every time a tenant moves out. I'll have the hardwood floors refinished in ebony or black stain. It's not cheap, but it's a long-term investment in the home. It covers most previous and future pet stains well, as I allow animals in all my rental properties. You can eliminate pet owners as renters, however this really will whittle away at your renter's market. Even if I had the floors refinished twenty years ago, I can still make them look great with products that are sold today. I have one company that I've been using for 15 years for refinishing hardwood floors, and they really know their craft.

I'm also a big believer in ceramic tile. I won't use laminate or some other cheaper option. It looks nasty and will not help the value of your property, so why do it? Remember, you've made a long-term investment when you purchased the property. Now that you're into the remodel process you don't want to start cutting corners. Do it right the first time, and it will look good many years down the road.

I search the center aisles at Home Depot and Lowe's, that's where they display the materials that aren't selling well. You can pick up materials in bulk for a 50% discount or more. I like the glass tile for back splash, and you can often find those for 50% off. They look great and add lots of visual appeal in the kitchen.

I use neutral colors. Eighty percent of my homes are painted in the same colors. I use a light grayish green color for interior walls. All cabinets and trim are painted in the brightest white I can purchase. I do this because it lets me take advantage of sales and purchase supplies in bulk at a big discount. I also don't want to have to do another remodel five years from now because I put up some kind of wallpaper or painted some walls mauve. I want it to be simple, clean, and basic.

I spend a lot of time with a paintbrush in my hand. Painting is the fastest and least expensive way to make a property look great. I've learned over the years what paint products work best. I also have the same colors in most of my properties so I don't confuse myself with trying to keep up with different colors for different properties. Keep things as simple as you can.

I always put granite counter tops in every remodel. I don't go to the places you see on HGTV. I go to discount granite dealers (you'll need to find one in your area). My granite contractor, who I use a lot, will let me know when new shipments come in so I can buy up a few sheets for properties later down the line.

I buy mostly black or charcoal grey granite. I don't buy super thick granite because it's too expensive. My last granite job was a little over $800 cut and installed. The people on HGTV shows would have spent $3000 on the same project and it doesn't make the house worth any more to you or your tenant.

I like the glass tile backsplash because it accentuates the granite. I can usually get those for $5 each on the sale rack at my two favorite hardware stores. When you advertise a home with granite counter tops it creates a lot of interest because everyone wants to go first class.

You'll probably need to remodel the bathroom(s). I usually buy older homes and try to stay as original as I can with things like bathroom tile. You can often clean up the old tile and make it look great. The original tile will often have a lot of character and suites the period and style of the home. If you have to replace the tile, go with something different than in the kitchen. You'll possibly be looking at retiling the bathtub/shower or use a tub kit. I prefer tile but the shower surrounds also work well.

Light fixtures come from Lowe's or Home Depot. Their pricing is much better than the specialty lighting stores and they have a good selection. You don't want to leave old nasty light fixtures in your home. They are very noticeable and you don't want to draw attention to a negative. Replace the light fixtures. Remember, you want the house to wow prospective tenants so you can get high rents and high quality tenants. You don't want to cut corners, or it will cost you in the long run.

I also like decks on homes. I like to expand the living space for my tenants and bring in the outside. I'll build a deck on the back and sometimes the front of almost every one of my homes. A nice deck can be added for minimal expense. It increases the visual appeal as well as adding perceived living space.

It's another great way to increase the value of your property while increasing the demand and value to perspective tenants.

Let's talk cabinets now. If you have to order new cabinets, make sure to order them 30 days out if they have to be made. I've made this mistake more than once. If you can salvage the existing cabinets and make them look more modern buy adding new hardware and crown molding, you can save yourself a lot of money. I'm going to remind you here that this is a sweat equity business. You create value buy doing your own labor when possible.

I provide the appliances for all my homes. Some of my colleagues in this business disagree with me on this but, when I advertise the home for rent, it draws a lot of interest when it is listed with granite countertops and stainless steel appliances. I do go through a lot of appliances. I want my homes to be higher end and bring higher rents so they need to be fully equipped. It's amazing how some stainless steel appliances can add big value for your perspective tenants. It's another amenity the competition isn't offering. Even more important, tenants will happily pay more for these amenities. I don't want mismatched ugly appliances in my home, and I assume my customers don't either.

I also provide washers and dryers in all my homes. I have a repairman that does a lot of work for me at reasonable rates to keep them up and running. He's a great part of my team and gives me great discounts for the amount of work I give him. Building a team is an important part of my business, which we'll talk more about later. For now you'll want to keep in mind that you will always be looking for talented people that will work with you. You provide lots of work, and they provide services that you can't do yourself. It's a win-win and vital to your long-term success.

I like to handle the lawn care for most of my properties. Once again, my colleagues disagree with me on this, but my past experience has shown that most tenants don't take very good care of their yards. This is a pet peeve of mine. I personally do the lawn care for several reasons. First, it helps keep me in good shape. Second, it helps me keep an eye on the properties so I can be proactive and catch things happening with the house before it becomes a big problem. It also allows me to create jobs for neighborhood kids of friends of mine.

Doing the lawns also keeps me out in the area, and I often spot new potential properties to buy while doing the yards. Another money saving investment I made was purchasing a lawn sprayer for weed control and pesticide. This has saved me approximately $3,300 per year over having the lawns sprayed. This investment also cuts down on the lawn care time. The big thing here is that I take a lot of pride in all my properties. I work very hard to make them beautiful inside and out, and I want them to stay that way. You would never pick one of my properties out as a rental. The tenants are typically happy with this arrangement and are more than willing to pay higher rents for this convenience.

I want to talk for just a minute about my hiring the kids of friends. Sometimes they don't make the cut. I don't have time for lazy kids, and they need to work at my pace. I have them sign a contract before they go to work for me, because I don't have time for them checking their phone all the time while they're working. We are there to get a job done and they need to understand that.

I don't want my properties to look like rent houses. It's important to me that my homes add value to the neighborhood rather than hurting the value. I bring value to the area by making my homes beautiful. I bring value to the community by hiring young people and teaching them how to work and the value of being able to use your hands to create beauty. Bringing value to the people around you is important, and I try to keep that in mind with everything I do.

Depending on your location, you may need to eventually invest in some tree cutting equipment. I didn't do this in the beginning and paid to have it done. It's hard to find this kind of service at any kind of discount, and I paid a lot of money to have trees cut out and trimmed. Tree contractors are very expensive and there is a lot of this work you can do yourself. I can use a pole saw and hand held chain saw and rent a hydraulic lift, which saves a fortune over hiring a contractor. Now, I will hire a contractor for the more dangerous jobs.

Most of the work will be trimming back trees, which is important. You have to keep those limbs off your house and power lines or they can cause a lot of damage. In my part of the country, trees, and squirrels have caused some of my biggest problems and created my biggest expenses for repairs. It's amazing how much damage squirrels can do to an unprotected home. You have to be proactive and fix potential problems before they happen.

FINDING PROPERTIES FOR CASHFLOW

IT'S TIME TO TALK ABOUT THE HOUSES I buy, how I find them and what I'm looking for. I've mentioned this throughout the book, but I think the topic is important enough to deserve its own chapter.

First and foremost, you have to understand what I'm looking for, and more importantly, what I'm not looking for. I'm not looking for homes that are up to date and in perfect condition. I'm not looking for houses that I can buy for $100,000 plus and rent them the next week. I'm not looking for a turnkey investment. In my mind there is no such thing as a turnkey investment in this game.

I'm looking for properties that I can rent for positive cash flow. The properties I want need work, updating, and modernizing. I look for these kinds of properties so that, through my own sweat equity, I can create a positive cash flow. You have to understand that I love the challenge of taking something old and ugly and making it new and beautiful. It's this love of making the property better that gives me the ability to buy at a good price.

Side Bar: I'm not going to tell you that my method is the only method that will work for buying properties for the purpose of creating income bubbles. It is however, the only method I know and use. It's the method that has proven to work for me for over twenty years. Take the information I give you and make it your own. My real interest is to open your eyes to the opportunity that is all around and to help you build your own financial empire of multiple income producing properties.

Once you understand what I look for, you can begin your own search.

By design, most of my properties are within a two miles radius of where I live. It's much easier and more cost effective for me to manage my properties because they are so close to my primary residence, Ground Zero!

Over the years I've become familiar with the 20's & 30's style of home and I've learned what to look for and what to avoid. These older homes are solidly built and the basic structure usually remains sound. I know that if the bones of the house are strong, the rest can be easily fixed or updated. This is key to the way I do my business.

Many of the homes I now own were homes I found as my wife and I took evening walks through our neighborhood. It's amazing what you see when you get out of the car and just walk the neighborhood. I look for homes that need new landscaping, paint, fence and TLC. They need the kind of work that will increase their curb appeal, making them easy to sell or rent. Yes, I said sell! I said it because, if the house has the kind of curb appeal that would make it an easy sell, then it will also be easy to lease for a higher monthly rent.

So, as I walk the neighborhood I always have my eye open for potential properties to buy. Maybe the house is run down, and it's empty. Maybe it's being cleaned out for whatever reason. I don't have to see a for sale sign in the yard to walk up and ask about the house. I've found some of my best properties this way, and it's a method I recommend you adapt.

Find an area in your town that is maybe close to you where the homes are older and possibly a little run down. Park your car and get out and walk the neighborhood. You can learn a lot about a neighborhood by walking the sidewalks. You can meet people in their yards and strike up conversations that can lead you to potential properties. You may see a home being remodeled. Walk up and ask about the house. You may find out the owner would love to get rid of it because they don't have interest in messing with it. Another person's problem could be your next income bubble.

After doing this for twenty years, I have a bit of an advantage. This is because I've purchased so many properties in my area, people know who I am and what I do. They know that when I buy a home, I make it one of the nicest looking homes on the street. So they never hesitate to let me know about a potential investment property. It wasn't always this way, but it's something to keep in mind as you start your business.

Another way I find properties is through my network of contractors and helpers. I've built a good network or team of people over the years. When they're not helping me, these folks are in homes working and fixing things for other people. They have access to finding possible investment properties for me; it's a win-win deal for everyone. They help me locate a new property, and if I buy that property they get more work as a result.

It's always important to keep in mind the value of the team you develop. We will talk more about building a team soon. For now you should keep in mind that everyone you know can be helpful to you. They can aid you in finding properties you'll be able to buy, which will create a new income bubble. So talk to everyone.

Let them know what you're doing. Look at houses, and study your market.

Of course there are plenty of other ways to find your properties. You can always go to Craigslist and the local newspaper adds. You can develop a relationship with a realtor who has access to the multi list. You can search Google for homes for sale in your area, but you must learn the market and determine the best area for you to find the kind of properties you seek.

This really isn't rocket science. It's going to take a little time and effort on your part. You'll have to do some homework to know your market and find the neighborhoods that are the best fit for you. If you follow my advice, you'll look for single-family homes that are older and relatively small. These homes can use a lot of work, and if you're willing to get your hands dirty, you can get into these homes for a big discount over a home that's up to date and move-in ready.

This is how I've built my business. I look for homes I can buy for typically $90,000 or less. My last investment cost $30K. I'll take that house and invest about $30K, as it needs the three "Bigs," electric, plumbing, and heat and air. After all cosmetics are done, this house should appraise in the mid $90's. I just added $30,000 to my net worth...and I do this several times per year. I will put this house on a 12 year note, or a 15 year note if my banker will let me. This will make the mortgage payment on this property $700 a month. Taxes and insurance will be another $150 per month, bringing the total monthly cost to $850. This rental will bring $1,095 per month or more, which gives me approximately $245 per month cash flow. You bet I'm going to spend some money and time fixing the house up to get it ready. It's going to take hard work and sweat on my part. That's okay because when I'm done, I'll have a home that will generate a good cash flow for as long as I own it. Since I haven't sold one yet, I'll own it for a long time. I'll still be in my early 50's when it's paid off. Just as the houses I purchased in my 20's were paid off in my 30's and the houses I bought in my 30's are now being paid off in my 40's. That's how you do it!

Remember that I do the remodel like I'm going to live in that house. I may spend more time and money on it in the beginning, but then it's done. After that it will only be quick fixes and inexpensive updates when a tenant moves out. That house is then ready to rent again for a higher monthly rent, which will give me a raise.

I know I keep harping on mindset, but repetition is a master skill, and I want to make sure you get the important lessons here. Look for homes that need work. Look for opportunities that are close to where you live so you don't have to travel all over the country to keep up with your properties. The closer you keep your properties to you, the better. Don't think about what it looks like now. Think about what it's going to look like when it's ready to rent. Do it right the first time, and you'll be able to get more rent for it. Neighbors will start to help you grow your business.

In the book The Seven Habits of Highly Effective People Steven Covey says, "Begin with the end in mind." In other words, create the vision of how you want your business to look 3, 5, 10 years down the road. Then start taking action one-step at a time. The reason I want you to see how I've built my business is so you can achieve what I've done faster and easier. So get that newspaper out and start doing your homework. Get out and walk around your neighborhood. If your neighborhood is too nice for this kind of model, then go across the street to the older neighborhood and walk that one.

There's nothing holding you back now except getting started.

THE FAST START MODEL

WE'VE TALKED ABOUT FINDING YOUR FIRST investment property. We've talked about the remodel and getting it ready to lease. Now it's time to talk a little about the best way to get into your property.

The easiest and cheapest way to get started in building your wealth with rental properties is to start by buying a small home and move into it. Fix it up and make it beautiful while you live there. Then buy another one and rent the first home. If you're young and just getting started, this is a great way to go.

You'll want to start small. I'm talking about buying a small two-bedroom one-bath home for $50,000. I've seen too many people start with more expensive properties and get themselves in trouble. Start small and learn as you go. Get that first house bought and fixed up. Then start looking for your next house as you're finishing up the first one.

This is a good way to get started because you get better interest rates and longer notes if you are buying as an owner occupant. Go with a thirty year fixed rate mortgage on your first few investments. This will allow you more cash flow because your payments are lower. You can get into a house with a minimum down payment and lower over all expense as an owner occupant. The down side is that you'll have to pack up and move when you're able to buy your next home. If you have a family, this can be very stressful on everyone. I didn't want to move every time I purchased a house. I was married and didn't want to get divorced. I did this once with my wife, and I can tell you we'll be in this home for the rest of our lives.

If you're not going to live in your house, you'll have to put 20-25% down to purchase the home. If you're not going to be the owner occupant, your interest rate will be higher. You'll need to put a significant amount down so you can create a positive cash flow from this new property.

Let's take the same scenario as an owner occupant. You buy an older two-bedroom one-bath home for $50,000. Hopefully this home is very close to where you live currently. If you put 20% down on the home, you're looking at $10,000 down plus closing costs. Closing costs could be around $1500 if you split the closing costs with the seller. Always try to negotiate closing costs.

Your total cost at closing is $11,500. By putting this much down on the house, you've eliminated having to pay for PMI (Private Mortgage Insurance). It's okay to pay PMI if you have to on your first house, but you don't want to keep doing that. It's a waste of your money. It was designed to protect the mortgage company. Your monthly payment is about $400-$500 a month. If you live in the house and fix it up, you'll have a nice house that can bring you good cash flow when you rent it. If you rent this house for $1,050 a month you'll be cash flowing $550 a month. That is $6,600 a year in positive cash flow. In this scenario you make up your investment in down payment and closing costs in two years. Most new cars cost as much as this house nowadays, and you'll never make positive cash flow on a new car.

Live in your house for two years. Why two years, you ask? The answer is capital gains. If you live in a home for 2 years and you decide to sell that investment later, you won't pay capital gains. This is why you need an accountant on your team. You spend time at night and on weekends fixing it up and making it beautiful. Your yard and landscape is the best on the street. Your home has curb appeal. You've made it beautiful and up to date inside and out. You have sweat equity in this home. It now appraises for considerably more than you paid for it, not to mention how you feel about your accomplishment and the skills and knowledge you've gained on your first project.

Now it's time to look for your second house. Once again you'll be purchasing your second house as an owner occupant so you can get into it with minimum money down and a better interest rate. As soon as you get into your second house, it's time to get the first one rented. My method is Postlets.com which will put your house on Trulia & Zillow, where people are already looking for you and you didn't even know it. Never put a "For Rent" sign in the yard of your property, it shows vacancy and you don't need a break in. I also put an ad on Craigslist, and get it rented. "If it's not makin' money its takin' money," and we're in the business of making money. This is why I provide necessary information on my website. You can download rental applications and all forms that you will need to rent this and all future properties at www.millionairemaintenanceman.com for free!

It's going to be hard to leave that first house. You've put your time and sweat into making it beautiful. I get attached to all my properties. It's hard to hand over the keys to someone after you've put all that work into a home. However, that's where you start building your wealth. Remember, the tenant is now your customer. The house, is and always will be, your baby. It gets easier to do, especially after you've had a tenant pay a house off for you and you are cash flowing over a thousand dollars a month on one of your properties.

Now when you find your second house, you want to see about refinancing the first house so you can get rid of the PMI insurance. I recommend that you look for a banker to work with you for your investment properties. Banks are asset-based lenders, and you now have assets.

A banker can get you better rates and if your house is worth more than you paid for it, and it should be, you can borrow some extra money to finance your remodel on the second house. You want to shorten the term of the note on the first house so it will pay off in as short of time as possible and still generate positive cash flow. When I get permanent financing on one of my houses, I could take out a 10-12 year note on the property, but I always ask for 15, because at 15, I get a much better cash flow. I've had many tenants stay with me that long and pay off the home for me.

You'll need to go through a mortgage company, not your banker, on the second house because that's the one in which you're going to live. Now you will live in your second house for two years while you're fixing it up, and then start looking for your third house. Again you'll want to refinance the second house and shorten the term of the note. You can suck a little money out of the second house to get your third house under way and eliminate the PMI on that one.

This is a simple process that works. Do it once, then rinse and repeat and build a massive portfolio of properties in just a few years. Think about it! I get $1000 a month or more for my houses. If you buy a house every two years, in ten years you'll have five houses. If you refinance each house on a ten to fifteen year note, you'll have paid off your first house. That means you'll be cash flowing over $1000 on that house alone, in addition to the other four houses you have rented.

If moving every time you buy a house isn't what you want to do, then you'll just have to be prepared to have a bigger investment up front when you purchase a property. If you've followed my advice and gotten rid of your debt, eliminated unnecessary expenses, and lived below your means, you should be fine. You'll just want to remember to start small. Don't take on more than necessary, at least in the beginning. If you follow my advice here, it won't be long and you'll be getting big in no time.

IT TAKES A TEAM TO CREATE SUCCESS

IS IT POSSIBLE TO CREATE SUCCESS without help? It might be possible, but I've personally never heard of it. In the famous book "Think and Grow Rich," one of the success principles was the mastermind principle. In other words, surround yourself with like-minded people that will help you, and in return, you help them.

This principle is put to work in every industry by the greatest minds in business and every other endeavor. This principle is a key factor in my own success in this business as well as my success in the corporate world. Without my mastermind group/team, I wouldn't have been able to create the kind of success I've enjoyed in my life. That's why I thought it was an important enough topic to devote a chapter of this book.

You'll want to form a relationship with key people. These people are going to be crucial to your success in this business. They are going to have expertise in areas you don't. Sure you can study and learn in an effort to be a one man or woman show. Why? Why would you distract yourself from the true goal? That goal is to buy a house, fix it up, make it beautiful, and get it rented for a high rent. Anything other than that is a distraction that will cost you money.

You can learn anything you want, and you'll get plenty of chances to learn in this business. You're going to learn volumes through your hard work and experience. If you follow my advice you'll also learn from your team. Your team will be made up of experts in areas that you don't excel. It would take you years of study, trial and error, and thousands of dollars in costly mistakes to learn what the people on your team already know.

You're going to learn a lot from your team members. You're going to need a few contractors on your team, and you'll need to learn as much as you can so you can talk to your contractors intelligently. You're going to be the project manager for each property that you purchase. You will be responsible for communicating with your team to make sure they are clear on what you want done. You will be the first one on the job site, and on most days, the last one to leave. This comes easy to me because in my corporate world job, I was used to herding cats. You may have the skill that you are better at managing people. Capitalize on YOUR strengths.

I tend to over explain to my team what and how I want the project done. I tell them up front what I expect. I also advise them to let me know if they have a better, easier way of doing something. I'm very fair with everyone on my team, and will never ask anything of him or her that I won't do. I expect quality work from the people I hire, and I don't accept anything less. This is my business and my passion, and it's important that it's done right.

I will hire friends and family. It's okay to hire them. I just don't do business with them like renting them a home. I've been through this in the past, and it doesn't work. I don't recommend it. I've hired a family member or a friend, and I've had to fire them. I won't hire them back if they don't perform. I pay well and expect a return on my investment. I feel like I'm a good employer. I take my team out to lunch all the time or bring lunch to them. Sometimes we'll even have a few beers at the end of the day.

Find your team members and marry them young! What do I mean by this? Some of my contractors are getting up there in years, and I'll need to find new contractors to replace them when they retire. I take good care of my people/team. Even the older guys tell me they'll take good care of me in retirement because we've become friends and enjoy working together. They've seen me grow my business and are proud of my accomplishments because they've been a key part of my success.

I have a team of two guys that have worked with me for twenty years. They can do anything. They can work concrete, tile, carpentry, plumbing, and heat and air. You name it, and they can do it. You have to abide by code in your area, so you'll have to have licensed professionals do the major stuff. The minor stuff is pretty easy, and these guys can handle most anything.

I love these guys, and they are like family to me. We've worked together for many years. When I didn't have work for them, I busted my butt to keep them working by promoting them to other people in my network. Their success is my success, and I've always taken that seriously. None of them are full time employees. They work for other people, and I do my best to get them as many jobs as possible.

Remember, I come from a white-collar corporate environment so I have a lot of contacts with people that need things done and don't have the time or ability to do it themselves. I get calls all the time because everyone knows that I have a sizeable network of general contractors.

People are always looking for a good heat and air person, plumber, or electrician. This way I'm able to get my team a lot of work. Sometimes I hurt myself, as they get so busy that I have to book them a couple of weeks in advance. That's okay with me because their success is my success.

I use my general contractors all the time. We're very good friends and enjoy working together. The neighborhood kid that helps me is also a major part of my team. He spends a lot of time with me in the summer months and on weekends during the school year. This kid is a hard worker and I went through a lot of kids before I found him.

I have a contract that I have the kids I hire sign before they come to work for me. The contract is about work ethic and my expectations. I've been an employer for a long time at a major company, and sometimes you need to go back to the basics. I give my employees a job description, and they have the opportunity to make up to $2.00 an hour more based on their work performance. I learned in the corporate world that the greatest dis-service you can do to an employee is to be unclear about your expectations. When I hire someone, they are clear on what I expect. They know if they don't meet those expectations, they won't get to work for me. It may sound hard, but it's the best thing you can do for a youngster. I teach these kids how to work and how to be proud of the work they do.

In the previous chapter I talked about the importance of developing a relationship with a banker. Your banker is going to be a major part of your team. Your banker is going to help you get your houses refinanced at a good rate so that you can generate positive cash flow from your properties while paying them off in a shorter time frame. Eventually, you may establish a line of credit that you use to get ownership of a property and fund the remodel. Then you get your permanent financing when the house is done and leased. This is how I do it now.

Another key person on your team will be your accountant. I've been with my accountant almost since the beginning. My accountant also owns rental properties so he knows my business as he's in the same business. My accountant has been an important part of my team for twenty years now and I talk to him on a regular basis. He has not only saved me money, but he's made me money and is an important part of my mastermind group.

It's never too early to start building your team. Start thinking about the areas that you can handle and the things you know you'll need help with. Start talking to people and get to know some people that might make good members of your team. You won't have a lot going on in the beginning, but over time you can reach a point where you can keep some people pretty busy. That's where I am now, and I could've never achieved this great success without my team.

LET'S TALK CONTRACTS

CONTRACTS ARE JUST A PART OF DOING business, and you shouldn't be intimidated by using a contract. You have to sign a contract to buy a house or a car. You have to sign a contract to borrow money. You sign contracts all the time. It's a part of everyday business, and it will be a part of your business.

I'm going to go over the contract I use for leasing my properties with you step by step. I want you to get a feel for what I include in my contract. Everything is there for a reason, and the contract is designed to protect both the tenant and myself. Not only am I going to go over my contract in this chapter, but I'm also going to give you a copy of the contract(s) I use at www.millionairemaintenanceman.com. I want you to be fully armed with the tools you need to start your business, and these contracts are key tools to have in your toolbox.

The contract that I use and suggest you use is a simple five page contract that covers every aspect of the transaction and responsibilities of the landlord and tenant. Over the years I've taken several contracts from several books or articles to develop my own. I'm going to hand this contract to you on a silver platter.

In my contract, I use the discount rent policy. If I list a property at $1250 a month and I sign the contract with the tenant, he or she has to pay me by the first of every month to remain at $1250 a month rent. I do this for one main reason. I know my tenants want to pay on time. Nobody wants to disappoint, and I understand that. However, when I make all the deposits, I sometimes get checks on the 1st, 3rd, 7th, etc. I was making several deposits each month. Payments are due on the 1st of every month. For example, say the rent is $1,300 per month, but if they pay on or before the 1st, they only pay $1,250. This is a bit of reverse psychology for the renter, but it works for me. If the tenants pay all year on time, in December their rent is reduced $50 as a Christmas bonus. It really makes them smile. I do make exceptions. If I have a tenant that has been on time for two years, and they make one mistake, I'm not going penalize them.

Article 7 of the contract "Use of the Premises" is there to protect you. This article states that the tenant will pay an additional $75 for each additional person. This will eventually happen to you. You'll lease your property to a single person or couple and a friend or family member will get down on their luck and move in. This puts more wear and tear on the property. I have some duplexes where I pay the water bill, and this will mean a jump in the water bill. If you don't have this in your contract, it'll cost you money.

Article 8 is about pets. My wife and I have pets. We have 4 dogs and 2 cats, so it's clear we are animal lovers. My wife donates a lot of money and time to animal charities, so I do allow pets in my properties. You'll have to make your own decision whether or not you'll allow pets. If you decide not to allow pets, I completely understand. However, you need to be aware that this will limit your potential market. You want your tenants to stay with you forever. You want them to hang pictures on the walls and have a pet if they desire. You want them to make your house into their home. I typically meet the dog before I let them into my house. I also make the tenant very aware that smells, disturbing the neighbors due to barking, or destruction to the property will get the animal evicted. Thankfully I've never had to do that, but I've sure thought about it. I have nice homes, and the tenants do a good job taking care of their animals. I also make the tenant pick up the dog poop out of the yard. I mow the yards of my properties and don't want to be stepping in dog poop.

Article 9 is Non Assignment, which means the tenant cannot sublet the property. This means they can't re-rent the property to another party without my approval. This can happen when a tenant needs out of a contract quickly. I understand that things happen and circumstances change. However, this is my property and I'm picky about the people I let live in my property. I have a big investment and this part of the contract ensures that I have a say in who is living in my house.

Article 10 is legal obligations. This is exactly what it sounds like. If the tenant doesn't pay me the rent, they will be in trouble.

Article 11 covers attorney costs. This says that the party that loses the action will be responsible for attorney costs. I have to be honest here. I've never had to go to court in my life. I've never had to sue anyone, and I've never been sued. I like to be proactive to any situation that may arise. If a tenant doesn't pay, you have to get them out of your property. That has happened to me several times. Yet I've never had to call the police to get a tenant out. I guess I've been very fortunate here. Even when I'm kicking someone out, I still treat them with dignity and respect as long as they don't avoid me. Persistence becomes omnipotent when you're dealing with a tenant that won't pay. You have to stay on top of the situation. I'll call them repeatedly. I'll go put notes on the doors. They know I'm watching them. You have the right to be pissed when you have an asset that you lease to someone and they're not paying you. You still have a mortgage on the property and no cash flow. If the property isn't making you money, it's costing you money. Most of the time when I put an eviction notice on the door, they move out pretty quickly. Just be aware this will happen, and you need to be prepared to be persistent and stay the course without being nasty.

Article 12 is about the repair policy and is part of the discount rent program. This is pretty simple. I don't want tenants calling me to change light bulbs and other minor maintenance tasks. If they stop up the toilet, they need to break out the plunger and get it fixed. I've never been asked to do that, but we do a lot of sewer line clean outs. No feminine products in the toilet period.

Article 13 pertains to basic tenant responsibilities and codes for the particular state. Each state will have their own codes regarding tenant responsibilities. You'll need to make these adjustments to the contract to work in your state. It's pretty simple, but you want to make sure your contract is within the guidelines of the state where you're operating.

Article 14 is about the security deposit. This is to cover any expenses that you incur while preparing the house for the next potential tenant. I refer to this as a "make ready" rather than a "remodel." I'm very clear with tenants about this. I want them to make this their home. Like I mentioned earlier, I want them to hang pictures and make it their place to live. If all I have to do is caulk a few holes where they hung some pictures and paint over them, the tenant will get their full deposit back. That doesn't always happen, but I have some people do a remarkable job. I give everyone my "definition of cleanliness" before they take possession. I turn the property over to them in pristine condition, and I expect to get it back in the same condition. If I don't get it back in that pristine condition, I charge them for it. If you don't open the oven till after the tenant is gone and there's 3 years of caked up crud all over the inside, you're screwed. This has happened to me, so I'm telling you now so you don't let it happen to you.

Article 15 talks about month-to-month tenancy. After the tenant has been in the house for one year, their obligation is up and they are then on a 30 day contract. This article covers them giving a 30 day written notice if they plan on vacating the property.

Article 16 covers removal of landlord's property. I provide carbon monoxide detectors, smoke alarms, and fire extinguishers for every property I have. Sometimes these are not all there when you get the property back and doing your "make ready." The bottom line with this article is, "Don't remove items from the property if you want to regain your deposit."

Article 17 talks about tenant insurance. I always highly recommend tenant insurance. Most of my properties are close to downtown Oklahoma City. All of the properties have alarms, but anytime you live in a major metropolitan area you have the potential for loss. Neither my insurance coverage, nor I as the landlord, will protect the tenant's personal belongings. That is up to the tenant.

Article 18 covers abandonment. This basically says that if the tenant leaves owing you rent, you take possession of the property and personal property.

Article 19 is the lock policy, which says not to change my locks.

Article 20 covers the condition of the premises. The tenant needs to report any problems to the landlord within three days of taking possession of the property.

Article 21 is about the inventory and inspection record. I have my own spreadsheet that I use to inspect my properties and take inventory of all the items that should be there. This is an important document, and I'll provide you with a copy of the one I use. You can make changes and adapt it to your needs as you go along, but it will make a good template for you to get started.

Article 22 covers tenant responsibility. Basically this talks about how the tenant needs to keep the house clean, not do any damage, and make sure to let me know of any potential problems as soon as they notice them. I view my tenants as my customers. I want to take good care of my customers to make them want to stay with me for many years. If they will take care of the house and let me know if they notice a potential problem, this gives me the chance to be proactive and fix something before it becomes an expensive repair.

Article 23 is about landlord responsibility. This means you will be responsible for maintaining the fence, plumbing, heating and air conditioning, electrical and mechanical systems, as well as the general structure and apperance of the property.

Article 24 covers alterations. I don't want a tenant painting in my home. They are typically too sloppy. I'll allow them to plant flowers and I'll even pay for them if they beautify the property. The landlord must approve any alterations.

Article 25 covers lawn maintenance. I mow all my lawns. This is another advantage of having most of my properties in a two mile radius of my home. It also allows me to be on site every week during the summer. I'm able to spot things that need attention and again be proactive which saves me a lot of money in the long run. I'm picky about the way my properties look. I want them to look beautiful and to be seen as an asset to the neighborhood. By mowing my own lawns I ensure the home looks great and my tenants appreciate not having to worry about it. If you don't want to mow your own yards, you need to be clear on you expectations with your tenants.

Article 26 is the vehicle policy. This covers no parking in the yard at all. I don't allow cars on cinder blocks in the driveway or commercial vehicles like big trucks. I also don't want RV's in the driveway of my properties. This is usually covered by the city codes and may be included if there's a neighborhood association. Putting the vehicle policy in the contract keeps any guesswork out of the equation.

Article 27 talks about utilities. I typically leave utilities as the tenant's responsibility. I do provide the tenant with all the phone numbers and contact information to get their utilities set up. I don't pay utilities except for the water bills of my duplexes.

Article 28 is the roof and termite alert. It's just telling the tenant to let me know if they have any leaks, evidence of rodents, or infestation of any kind.

Article 29 is about non-liability. This is telling the tenant not to do anything that could harm themselves. In other words, don't get up on the roof of the house to check a leak. That's when they need to call me, and I'll take care of it right away.

Article 30 is the disclosure of landlord agent. This article means that I can have other people do work on the property on my behalf.

Article 31 is the validity of lease provisions. This means that if anything changes in the law, we have to abide by that change and make a change to the contract.

Article 32 talks about access to the premises. If for any reason I need to get into the house, I always give the tenant a 24-hour notice.

Article 33 is a waiver. It's important to have a place to put everything down in writing. Don't leave anything to guess work. This is your house and your business. Guesswork can wind up being very costly.

Article 34 explains the terms, which is legal language for the contract.

Article 35 talks about full disclosure. Full disclosure means that I have not withheld any information to my knowledge about the property.

There you have it. This is the contract that I use. I have the tenant initial each page and sign the back with their social security number. This contract has worked well for me over the years, and I highly recommend that you download a copy of it and use it in your business. It would be wise to have your attorney look it over because there may be language required for your state. It's free to you, and I hope you'll use it to build your business.

MARKETING FOR SWARMS
OF HIGH QUALITY TENANTS

FIRST, I WANT YOU TO GIVE YOURSELF a pat on the back for coming this far. If you've read all the way through and taken action along the way, you're closer to actually having additional income bubbles and changing your life. If you're still on the fence about the whole thing, you might want to ask yourself a couple of questions.

Ask yourself if not taking action is moving you toward your goals or away from them. Understand that nothing stands still. Every thought either moves you toward or away from where you want to go. If you want to change your life, leave your job, or build financial freedom, you are going to have to take action.

So what is it that's keeping you from taking action? These are questions only you can answer.

Whether you follow my example or choose another path toward achieving the life you desire, these are questions that you need to think about in order to move forward. One thing is for sure. If you continue to do what you've always done, you'll continue to get what you've always gotten.

With that, let's move on. It's time to talk about marketing your property. You've spent your time and money to get into your property and make it beautiful. You've poured your blood and sweat into this thing, and you've turned it into a beautiful home where anyone would be proud to live. Now it's time to start generating revenue from all your efforts.

When we talk about marketing, a lot of people start to run the other way. They start thinking sales, and then they get all freaked out that they might have to sell something. So let's deal with this thought process before we go any further.

You are a salesperson whether you know it or not. You are selling every day of your life. And if you're not selling, you're buying what someone else is selling. That may sound a little harsh, but it's true. Let me ask you something. Have you ever recommended anything to a friend? Have you ever told someone about a great movie, book, or restaurant? Are you married, or do you have a significant other? Well guess what? You've sold, and someone bought what you were selling.

Nothing happens in our world until something is sold. If you convinced an employer to hire you, you've sold. If you convinced your spouse to marry you, you've sold. If you've ever talked someone into trying something new, you've sold. You're selling all the time, and it's not bad or evil.

If you want to make money in business, you have to sell. You can build the biggest, best widget ever built, but if you never sell one, it won't make you rich or help anyone else. Selling isn't the used car guy with the gold tooth, handle bar mustache, and high pressure.

Selling or marketing, in this case, is simply presenting your product or service in the best possible way. It is to entice your target market to take action and focus on the facts, features, and benefits of that product. The action we want is for someone to pay you what you want monthly for your home.

This home that you've put all your work and effort into is something of beauty and will benefit the people that live in it. There is nothing bad or sleazy about it. It's the way the world works, and if you want to make money at anything, you need to be ready to market/sell what you have.

Okay, now that we've got that out of the way, let's talk about how we are going to drive high quality tenants to your properties. I've been doing this for twenty years now, and I rarely have a property that takes more than a few days to get leased. Often times, they lease within hours. Keep that in mind because I charge a premium for my properties. So if I can get premium rent for my properties, you can too.

For years, I've used mostly Craigslist to market my properties and have had great success with it. It costs you nothing to post an ad on Craigslist, and it's a huge market place with a lot of traffic. It's a great way to list your properties with no cost out of your pocket. The downside is that you can get a lot of tire kickers and lookers that aren't qualified or capable of paying the rent you will be charging. There is a way to minimize this issue though. The way to keep this to a minimum is in the way you write your ad. I'll show you what I mean in a minute, but first let's talk about your ad and some of the basics.

The first step in attracting the right tenants is your headline or title to your ad. Whether your ad is on Craigslist, the local newspaper, or any other medium, you want your title to be clear and complete. I start my titles with the amount of rent I'm expecting for the property. This eliminates the tire kickers and the people that can't afford your property. Remember, you don't need a lot of lookers, you just need a few that are qualified to pay what you're going to charge.

I also list the basic features of the property in the title. I list the monthly rent, the number of bedrooms, square footage, and address. This information will give prospective tenants what they need to know to make a quick decision of whether or not they need to read further. If the home is priced out of their range, too big, too small, or in the wrong location, you've eliminated most of the folks that aren't your target market. You've also captured the attention of the folks that are your target market, and they are the focus.

You've heard the old saying that a picture is worth a thousand words. That is especially true when you are marketing your rental properties. Now that we have our headline, we want pictures. The more pictures you have in your ad the better. You'll want pictures of the inside as well as the outside. Anything that might be considered a benefit is worthy of a picture. If your house has a nice front porch, get a picture. If you have a nice back yard or a wood deck, you'll want a picture.

Now that you've got your pictures, we need to lay down the ground rules for our perspective tenants. This is where you state things to satisfy questions a prospective tenant may need to know. You should list whether or not pets are allowed. State whether or not you will allow smoking.

Now it's time for you to list all the features of your property. You should list things like, fenced back yard, wood deck, granite counter tops, hardwood floors, garage, monitored security system, faux wood blinds, etc. You'll also describe the area. So if your property is ten minutes from downtown, tell them this in the ad. If it's close to a school, tell them in the ad. You want to let the prospective tenant know as much as possible from your ad. If you do a good job here, the rest of the job will be a breeze. It will also eliminate a tremendous amount of unwanted phone calls.

The more complete and detailed you are in your ad, the faster you'll be generating positive cash flow from your property. I can tell you that if you shortcut your ad, you will not command a higher price for the property. It's just a fact. The more detail you have, the more likely you are to command a high price for the property.

> Writing a detailed ad will always bring higher prices whether you're leasing a house or selling old clothes on eBay. If you don't believe me, test if for yourself. I promise you'll be amazed.

So, put all the detail you can in your ad. Anything you can think of is worth mentioning. If you're marketing on Craigslist, there is no fee for more words in your ad, so take advantage of that.

Here is an example of the ad for one of my most recent properties. This property was on the market only a couple of days, and the new tenants are thrilled.

Notice the detail of the ad and all the features listed. If you write a detailed ad and have good pictures that show your house in the best possible way, you'll have your home generating positive cash flow in no time.

$1395 / 2BR - 1200FT^2

STUNNING, NEWLY REMODELED HISTORICAL

2BR / 1 Ba 1200ft house available now, w/d in unit detached garage, no smoking, cats are OK - purrr dogs are OK - wooofVery large 2 bed 1 bath 1200 sq ft. This house is fully loaded with all stainless steel appliances including dishwasher, over mount microwave, refrigerator, glass top stove, and washer & dryer. Granite countertops with stainless steel under mount sink. Glass tile backsplash and lots of cabinet space. Newly refinished hardwood floors throughout. Ceiling fans in both bedrooms & living room. This historical home has been brought back to its original beauty with modern amenities. Complete 6 foot stockade privacy fenced back yard. 2 car detached garage with electricity. Large covered front porch. Faux wood blinds throughout. CH&A. Electric fireplace with heat. Monitored security system. 2 blocks from OCU; $7 cab ride to downtown/Bricktown. Lawn care included. Pets okay with landlord's discretion; smoking is not allowed inside. $1,395 deposit, $1,395 monthly rent with 1 year minimum contract.

Do NOT contact me with unsolicited services or offers

Use my ad shown above as a template for every ad you place for your properties. You'll keep your properties rented and generating cash flow for many years to come.

Now it's time to take what we've learned and put it all together...

PUTTING IT ALL TOGETHER

—▬▬ ▬▬—

I'VE TALKED ABOUT A LOT OF GOOD information in this book. When I started putting this book together, the goal was to give you everything you need in order to get off the couch and start taking action.

I wanted you to see that your past doesn't matter. It doesn't matter what you've done or haven't done. The past is the past. There's nothing you can do about the past. The only good thing about looking back is to get clues to prevent you from making the same mistakes. Learning from past experience is a positive way to make the past work for you.

You also can't change your life by spending all your time thinking about the future. I know you may read that and think, "What the hell is he talking about?"

Here's what I mean. If you spend all your time thinking about the future, you'll never get anything done. The only time that matters is right now. What are you going to do with the time you have right now in the present?

You shape your future by the actions you take or don't take in the present. You can dream, plan, and think about something from now forward, but nothing happens. Nothing changes until you take action, and that has to be done in the present. If you think about it, it makes sense. I'm asking you to get your mind in the present and figure out what action you can take right now that will move you in the direction of your goals for the future.

If you've read this far, it's because something in this book makes sense to you. You can see how this worked for me and how it can work for you. Something in your gut is telling you to get off the couch and do something, take some kind of inspired action, and get the ball rolling.

You don't have to have all the answers. You don't have to know each step in the process. You don't have to really know anything more than determining your first step. If you have debt, then sit down and look at your debt and develop a plan to get rid of it. Sell anything you don't need anymore. Look at downsizing to free up your cash. Take inventory of your assets, so you know where you are now. Then you can devise a plan to take you where you need to go to start changing your life.

All I'm asking is for you to take that first step. Maybe start looking at properties in your area. Start getting a feel for the kind of rent that is being charged. Study the 'Houses for Rent' section of the Sunday paper. Look on Craigslist and see what is available and what they're charging. Start doing your due diligence.

Every step you take will move you closer to your goals. On the other hand, if you take no action, what will your life be like five years from now? What about ten years from now? Taking action is the only way you will change your life. It's the only way you'll create wealth and a lifestyle of freedom for yourself and your family.

You can do this if you choose, but only if you get started. There is a difference between the 1% that becomes wealthy and the 99% that live their lives broke or almost broke. The difference is, the 1% that becomes wealthy, take consistent action to achieve their goals.

They know they'll make mistakes, and they know that the success they desire is just on the other side of those mistakes. They don't spend time with worry and fear. Why? Because they're too busy taking action. The fastest cure to procrastination, which is a symptom of fear, is taking action.

I've shown you that I'm not the smartest guy in the world, and I've shown you my fears: heights, bugs, coconut, and especially the mechanical monkey with clanking symbols...all that scares me. I couldn't even pass the ACT to get into college to accept a football scholarship. I've shown you that I'm human and have made mistakes along the way. Hell, I'm still making mistakes everyday. I love mistakes because every time I make a mistake, I learn something. So I get to begin again more intelligently.

I showed you that I learned to work on my own properties. I learned by watching HGTV and YouTube videos. We are so fortunate today because no matter what you need to learn, there's a YouTube video that will show you how to do it. I learned, and I keep learning. I've created an amazing life for myself because I always take action instead of getting caught up in fear and worry.

I can do anything I want to do. I have the money to go where I want to go and do what I want to do. The funny thing is, I don't really want to go and do anything different. I love what I do. I've been blessed to start a hobby of taking ugly old houses and making them beautiful. Over time I've been able to turn my hobby, which I love, into a business. This business has allowed me to live debt free and never again have to worry about a job or employer.

I really want the same things for you. I could've rocked along and never written this book and been fine. In fact, I had a lot of people advise me not to write this book. Something in me has always questioned whether what the crowd says is best. I knew that if one person read this book and was inspired to take action to change their life, all the effort and expense of writing it would have been worth it. I took action in writing this book against the advice of others, and isn't that what we've been talking about?

I love what I do and will probably keep doing this as long as I'm able. I can't think of a thing I'd rather do. So when people ask me how many houses I plan to own? My answer is, "As many as I can." That's just the way I feel about it. I understand that everyone may not want to work as hard as I do. I understand that everyone may not want twenty or more properties. That's fine.

Just imagine for a minute how owning two, three, or four houses would change things for you. What if you stopped with four houses? You buy, remodel, and rent them. After a few years, those four houses are paid for and you still have them rented. Now, how does it feel to have an extra $4000 or more coming in each month? I'm asking you to stop for a minute and just imagine how that would feel.

Folks, I know you had to buy the book, but the wealth of knowledge that this book contains is definitely worth the money that you paid. I've included free contracts, a rental agreement, eviction notices, etc. This is everything you need to get started and beyond. You can even search YouTube for my DIY videos.

I think you'll agree that even a few properties can completely change your financial picture over time. So please don't just read this and set it on a shelf to collect dust. If you can see yourself doing this, take action. If you think it's not for you, but you know someone that this could help, give the book to him or her and encourage them to take action. Either way, you'll make a difference, and that's what we're all here to do.

I HOPE YOU HAVE A PROFITABLE DAY!

SPECIAL THANKS

Craig Barton, Esq.
Patti Duran
Dale East
Jen Fisher

Made in the
USA
Lexington, KY